S0-CBX-250

BIRDS
BIRDS
BIRDS
BIRDS
BIRDS
BIRDS
BIRDS
BIRDS
BIRDS

HAMLYN

LONDON · NEW YORK
SYDNEY · TORONTO

CONTENTS

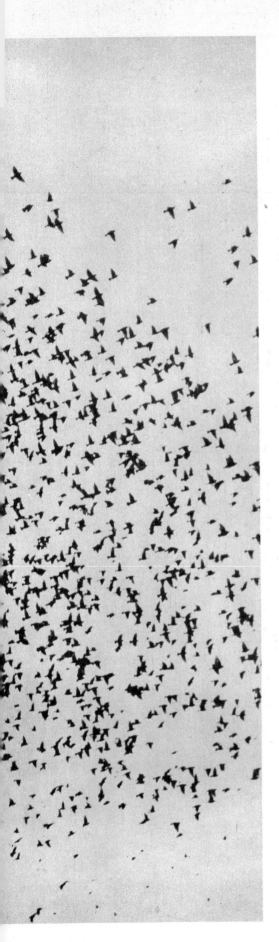

Published by **THE HAMLYN PUBLISHING GROUP LTD**
LONDON • NEW YORK • SYDNEY • TORONTO
Hamlyn House, Feltham, Middlesex, England
© Copyright 1965 Paul Hamlyn Ltd

ISBN 0 600 00461 9

First edition 1965
Fourth impression 1970
Printed in Czechoslovakia by Svoboda, Prague.
T 2131

BIRD BEHAVIOUR

BRUCE CAMPBELL

The Gannet's aggressive reaction to any trespasser is to open its wings and threaten with its spear-like bill.

Many birds develop special feathers in the breeding-season. Except for display these feathers may be quite useless: indeed they may be so large as to be an encumbrance. Often they are strikingly coloured. A familiar example is the splendid tail of the male Common Peafowl, the Peacock, with its magnificent train of iridescent green sheens and striking 'eye-spots' of gorgeous blue and bronze.

'Look at those two Curlews; they're walking very oddly.' We were standing on the footbridge at Montrose railway station, commanding one of Scotland's best bird-watching haunts, the basin of the South Esk. My friend is not a regular ornithologist, but something about the behaviour of the Curlews had caught his attention. I put up my telescope and for the next twenty minutes we watched as they strutted side by side, legs stiff, bills pointed downward, then stopped to peck at the mud. One bird looked larger, with the nape of its neck fluffed out and wings drooping below the tail — the cock, we presumed. From time to time he approached the hen and suddenly swung his body through a right angle; or she would make a quick run towards him, but without making contact. Twice he picked up and dropped little cockle-shells, but gradually the pair began to feed in earnest and their performance came to an end.

The striking feature of much bird display is its formal character, which had immediately impressed my friend. You do not have to be an expert to realize that here is a ritual distinct from the normal activities of the species. These ceremonies are often described as though they alone constituted 'bird behaviour', but this is misleading because birds are behaving all their lives and it is not always easy — in spite of what I have just written — to discriminate between an action which is still primarily functional, which we may call a 'routine', and one that has a secondary intention, a true display. One September evening as I was walking down a Welsh valley, about thirty House Martins flew out like a cloud of huge gnats from two cottages where they had been

This Blackcap, a common and widely distributed Old World warbler, is threatening a rival male which has entered its nesting-territory.

nesting. What was the motive behind this mass action, which looked curiously like the 'dreads' of terns or sea-swallows, when all the birds of a colony suddenly sweep out over the sea and back again on to their nests? The terns are usually silent; my House Martins called excitedly, but the movement was the same. Do they indeed 'dread' the swift attack of an enemy and bunch together to avoid it, or are they obeying a communal urge serving an end still obscure to us?

At present we explain much of the behaviour of other animals — and a good deal of our own — as the operation of inherited instinct producing a fixed reaction to a particular stimulus; and we believe these instinctive patterns have been evolved because they give the best results, in terms of survival, to the animal. As a simplified example: suppose you keep a number of sparrows in a huge aviary and introduce a pair of sparrowhawks. The sparrows which do not fly away or hide in thick cover will soon be caught and killed. If this situation continues indefinitely you will have a population of sparrows which survives because of the ability of most of its members to keep out of the hawks' way. All the young of alert and wary sparrows are not similarly endowed, but enough of them will carry the inheritance of those qualities to dominate the population, provided that the hawks continue to weed out the less efficient birds. Of course, it is also possible that young birds imitate their parents, so that each generation in turn acquires abilities that are useful to it. This is a form of learning and it is sometimes very difficult to disentangle its results from those of instinctive behaviour.

This young Horned Owl, disturbed whilst roosting in thick undergrowth, chooses offence as the best method of defence. Glaring at the intruder with its fierce, orange eyes, the pupils dilating and contracting, wings arched defiantly and feathers fluffed up to give an impression of greater size, it also hisses and snaps its bill.

7

The Mallards or Wild Duck in many English river valleys build their nests in the pollarded heads of old willow trees. This gives safety both from enemies living on the ground and from spring floods. But pollarding has only been practised since man began to tame the valleys — at the most a thousand years ago. So, although nesting in a pollard gives an advantage over nesting on the ground, it is unlikely that there has been time for the tendency to become part of the instinctive inheritance of the ducks by means of natural selection, and it is more probable that each duckling carries a memory of the site where it was hatched and looks for a similar one when its turn comes.

Some instincts are so bizarre that it is hard to see how they can have been evolved through natural selection. How did the European Cuckoo and the American cowbird come to abandon nest-building in favour of dropping eggs in other birds' nests? And how did their different methods develop? The Cuckoo ejects its broodmates one by one; the baby cowbird suppresses them by its superior size and ability to corner the food brought by the foster-parents. But we have to remember that most kinds of birds have been in existence for some millions of years and that their behaviour patterns have been perfected very slowly over countless generations.

During this long process certain movements have become specialized or ritualized, sometimes so remarkably that their origins are lost or obscured. When a male Rook presents his mate with a stick, we can see that what was originally a nest-building action now has a secondary function in forming or strengthening the bond between the pair. But

LEFT A Song Thrush, resenting the intrusion of a Starling, lowers its head and stretches out its neck in a threat-posture.

RIGHT The aggressive display of the lyrebird, in which the enormous spread tail plays a prominent part.

Two rival Chaffinches fighting out a territorial dispute. Males of many species such as this, though living in flocks and behaving amicably during most of the year, hold territories in the nesting-season which they jealously guard against any other males. Defence of a territory is often vital, for if it is lost to a rival the intruder may capture the female, too!

where did the crazy dances over the surface of the lake which are part of the display of the American Western Grebe spring from, or the frightening poses adopted by many game birds to threaten their rivals?

Broadly we can say that, whatever their origins, the displays of birds are concerned with critical moments in their lives, with courtship and mating, with aggression, with defence of food, territories or nests, or with frustrations of some kind, when the normal response to a stimulus cannot be made. We can usually recognize them because of the exaggerated postures involved, because movements are often repeated to definite patterns and because they may be accompanied by special calls and song. Displays associated with courtship and aggression are sometimes surprisingly alike; the classic example is provided by the European Robin: for years it was believed that the puffing out of the red breast feathers and the swaying from side to side on a perch were part of its courtship, until David Lack showed that they were aggressive postures between rivals.

Frustration displays often resemble routine movements: feeding, preening, or putting the bill under the wing as when sleeping. They occur when a bird, say, is prevented from returning to its nest by a human intruder and falls back on another type of activity altogether. We are as prone to this sort of display as the birds: anxiety makes some people bite their nails — false feeding — while others start yawning — false sleeping!

In general a bird's life, whether it is social or solitary, follows a regular and predictable course in which routines and displays are mingled. It wakes in response to increasing light or the calls of other birds, and may sing for a few minutes if it is in occupation of a territory; then, obeying the internal stimulus of hunger, it goes in search of food. Here acquired information may play some part in directing its search; but many young sea-birds are left to fend for themselves by their parents, showing that even feeding behaviour may be instinctive.

The inner bird reports when enough food has been taken, and perhaps increasing warmth is the next stimulus, leading to preening on a perch exposed to the sun. Sun-bathing postures — stretching the wings and tail — may also be a response to a hot surface and suggest those curious activities, smoke-bathing and anting, in which, it seems, routine and display meet. True anting, which has so far only been identified among perching birds, involves an exaggerated forward extension of the wings and the rubbing of the primary flight feathers — and apparently no others — with ants picked up in the bill. Anting and smoke-bathing may help to clear the bird of external parasites but they also seem to give a bird's equivalent of sensual pleasure, leading some to credit them with a sexual significance.

Supposing one bird's day is in early spring and he is a male, the sight of a female, after he has fed and preened, stimulates him to a series of displays of growing intensity, each one linked to the next until the final coition. The display of the Curlews which we watched at Montrose took place in autumn, and, though I believe it was part of a ritual leading to mating, it did not achieve more than the preliminary stages. There is an interesting revival of sexual activity among birds around the autumn equinox of the north temperate zone. Sometimes, if the season is exceptionally mild, eggs are laid and broods reared; usually there is song and mild courtship display, and species like Rooks and Starlings refurbish their nests.

Early in the year, the males or pairs of flocking birds only sort themselves out for part of the day, returning to the group to feed and sleep. As the light wanes, the flock responds by behaviour leading to roosting, perhaps by complicated aerial manoeuvres or preparatory gatherings, before settling into the chosen dormitory for the night.

The breeding season follows a predetermined course on the same lines as the daily routine. The pair bond formed, the female enters the territory already won by the male, probably after vigorous displays or actual fighting with rivals. Here he may show her several possible nest sites, sometimes performing a special display. The Pied Flycatcher, after singing and strutting near a tree-hole to attract the female, pops inside and pokes out his head with its prominent white frontal patch or spots. But I have seen one singing by a blind hole which he could not possibly have entered; if he had persuaded a female to approach, she would soon have rejected him. When there is a failure of this kind in the chain of reactions, instinct can offer no solution. Males which fail to get mates go on singing until their very songs become a danger to them, giving away their presence to enemies. This is the harsh rule of natural selection, falling equally on the unlucky and the inefficient.

The successful male persuades the female to take a site — or she may choose it herself within his territory — and building begins, with or without his assistance. Experiments have shown that the process is largely instinctive, each stage succeeded by the next with perfect

Large and sometimes clumsy-looking Mute Swans perform a graceful greeting display, signifying mutual recognition, as they push their heavy bodies out of the water by paddling with webbed feet, twisting their long necks, waving their heads and stroking one another's feathers with their beaks.

ABOVE Kittiwakes, cliff-nesting gulls found on both sides of the North Atlantic, have a gentle greeting ceremony which is performed almost throughout the nesting season, caressing the head and neck feathers of each other with their bills often with vocal accompaniment.

A pair of Razorbills greeting each other on a cliff-edge outside the recess in which they have their single egg.

precision. Sometimes — the Common Wren of Europe (Winter Wren in North America) is a good example — the male builds the exterior structure and the female lines it; sometimes both take part in all stages; often the male just accompanies his mate, while the males of some species may not even know where their wives are nesting.

The variety of nest sites, from the bare rock ledge of the Guillemot or Murre to the elaborate cradles of tailor birds, weaver birds and Long-tailed Tits, show how birds have adapted themselves to every kind of physical niche. There are the enormous mounds of the Australian megapodes in which the eggs hatch, like those of reptiles, in the heat of their surroundings, the excavated holes of Kingfishers and Bee-eaters, the edible brackets of the cave-dwelling swiftlets of the Far East, the fragile grass cups of the Old World warblers and the hanging leaf to which the African Palm Swift glues her two eggs.

The size of the clutch of eggs laid by each species may be governed by various factors: for some it is the largest number which the sitting bird can cover, for others it is the number of young which can be most successfully reared at one time on the food available. One egg fits the mangrove branch on which the Fairy Tern sits precariously, four meet point to point under the slim Snipe, but the comfortable Pheasant or duck can manage a dozen or more. Most small birds of the north temperate zone can fill four to six mouths; in the tropics it may be only two or three, but several broods can be raised through the year.

When the clutch is laid, there are further permutations on the parts played by the parents, from incubation by the female alone, through

A pair of Common Terns bow and call to each other in the early stages of pair formation, which eventually leads up to mating.

12

During mating the female nibbles at the throat feathers of her mate.

various proportions of sharing — sometimes the female sits by day and the male by night — to the group of Arctic waders whose males take over entirely. Is this last, as has been suggested, a device to allow the female, the egg layer, to escape being caught by an early winter?

The care of the young is equally varied in provenance, with two major divisions: those birds, like the ducks, game birds and waders, whose young can feed themselves as soon as they are dry, and those which have to be fed in the nest — with an intermediate group, including the gulls and terns, whose chicks are semi-dependent. The chain of reaction operates for the chick from the moment it stirs in the egg; once hatched, the blind young thrush strains its skinny neck towards the sound of the food-bringing parent — and will do the same to a human finger. The dainty little Avocet sweeps the shallows with its tiny bill a few hours after breaking out of the shell. At this early stage the young of geese and ducks are particularly susceptible to 'imprinting', the acceptance of the first living creature they see as parent. (Shakespeare interpreted the process slightly differently when Puck bewitched Titania!) Imprinting is not as hard and fast as was at first believed, and can occur later in life and involve inanimate objects: a bereaved Chinese Goose adopted a wheelbarrow when she lost her gander; when the wheelbarrow was in use, she transferred her attachment temporarily to the back wheel of a car.

Flight seems a skill that above all must be learned: how many pictures have there been of a row of baby tits and a parent alongside, with the caption 'The first lesson'? Yet a young pigeon, reared in

The display of the Sage Grouse of North America is one of the most astonishing of all. The male in full regalia, moved by the thoughts of love, prepares to make his advances . . .

. . . by blowing up two air-sacs in front of his neck until they are the size of tennis-balls, drooping his wings and bringing them forward, assuming an air of great self-importance . . .

. . . spreading out his huge tail feathers . . .

. . . he allows the air to escape from the sacs, producing a series of almost grotesque rumblings, wheezings and gurgles. This must be important, though the hens often appear to be completely unmoved.

captivity with confined wings, flies when its feathers are grown as strongly as one reared in freedom. It is probable, however, that skill is improved by imitation and most birds of prey have to learn from adults before they become proficient hunters.

I can well recall, as a boy bird-nesting in a Hampshire marsh, how I came on a Reed Bunting writhing and struggling among the sedges. I rushed after it, expecting to catch an injured bird, but it kept eluding me until I realized I was the victim of a very old trick. My father, wise to this, had meanwhile found the well-hidden nest in its tussock. A number of ground-nesting birds from different families — ducks, waders, game birds, as well as buntings and pipits — have evolved these 'distraction displays'. Some tree-nesters, for example the Turtle Dove, also use them, and they are most intense when the young are just hatching or hatched. The adult does not really run much risk in luring the intruder away, and it is easy to understand the development of behaviour which has such a definite function. But nature seldom settles for a uniform solution: the Lapwing or Peewit occasionally performs a distraction display, but much more often leaves her nest or young and returns to mob you violently. Arctic Skuas tumble about wildly at a distance and if this does not do the trick move into the attack.

Mobbing is not usually ritualized: it is a direct routine which may or may not be pressed home against the enemy. But there are stylized inherited displays designed to thwart him, such as the really terrifying attitudes of young Long-eared Owls, heads sunk between fanned wings and bills clicking. The young of several kinds of woodpecker set up a buzzing like a swarm of bees — a dual purpose effort also stimulating the parent to feed them, while brooding titmice dart their heads and 'spit' like snakes at inquisitive fingers.

When the young owls make their menacing stand, their co-operation is involuntary, a common reaction to an outside stimulus. But to what extent do birds work together to mutual advantage? Nest-building by both parents is an example governed by instinct. Others come from feeding: in the hunting routine of the skuas, one attacks a gull or tern until it drops its fish, which the second pirate catches and swallows. A careful kitchen-sink observer watched a Starling pull up the string of a hanging container until its companion could get at the food; then they changed places and repeated the performance. It is difficult to exclude intelligent learning from this sort of behaviour. But what about the group-living Acorn Woodpecker of western North America? The birds stud a chosen tree with perhaps thousands of holes in which they store acorns and, when these give out, stones.

Lastly comes the question many people ask about all animals: is there any room in their lives for play? Watch a Kestrel as it lazily avoids the attacks of a party of Rooks, an agile bandit defying the heavy-winged posse; tiring of the game, it streaks off in effortless beats, and you have one answer: play is often practice for something sterner. But the Starlings that slid down a snowy roof, the Eider Ducks that repeatedly shot the rapids, can we deny them the feeling of pure enjoyment we know ourselves and which seems to us the most innocently 'animal' part of our complex make-up? Even lives so closely governed by instinct as those of birds may be allowed moments not entirely directed to survival.

Peacock with outspread tail, displaying by preading it into a gigantic fan.

Barn Swallow

NORTH AMERICAN BIRDS

CHARLES E. HUNTINGTON

BIRD DISTRIBUTION

Because they are warm-blooded, because they can fly, and because they migrate over long distances, birds are more widely distributed over the earth's surface than any other group of animals except man. Yet they are not uniformly distributed, and the various species vary enormously in the extent of the ranges which they inhabit. The Peregrine Falcon breeds on all the continents except Antarctica and on many islands, while the Ipswich Sparrow of Sable Island, off Nova Scotia, is one of a number of species whose precarious existence is limited to a few square miles.

Why is a given species of bird found in one area and not in another? The reasons are of two kinds: there are factors which prevent a bird from immigrating to a place and other factors which prevent it from becoming established even if it should immigrate. Some birds, especially ground-dwellers like grouse, turkeys, pheasants, and chickens, are incapable of long flights and therefore are restrained by fairly narrow barriers in the form of bodies of water, mountains, deserts, or otherwise unsuitable country. Other birds seem extremely reluctant to make flights over strange terrain, even though they are physically capable of doing so with ease; in the Amazon Basin rivers only a few hundred yards wide form apparently insuperable psychological barriers to certain birds. Even when birds have crossed a barrier and invaded a land where their kind has not been before, the odds are heavily against their colonizing it. In the first place they cannot become established unless there is adequate food, nesting sites, and

The Red-tailed Hawk is one of the commoner American buzzards nesting widely in Canada and the United States. Birds breeding in the north migrate south in the fall. All buzzards, like the one in this photograph, spend much time soaring round in wide sweeps on the thermals, only occasionally giving a lazy wing-flap.

PRECEDING PAGE The Bald Eagle, emblem of the United States of America, is one of the finest birds-of-prey in the New World. Only a small population now remains and the majority of pairs fail to hatch out any chicks.

20

The Long-eared Owl – its 'ears' are really nothing more than tufts of feathers – is found in many of the temperate zones of the northern hemisphere. It is remarkably slim for an owl and has an eerie call – a moaning, plummy hoot thrice repeated. It is strictly nocturnal in its habits and is therefore more often heard than seen. In winter up to a score or more may share a communal roost by day.

TOP RIGHT The Sparrowhawk of North America is rather unfortunately named, not only because it leads to confusion with the Sparrowhawk of Europe, but because it is not really a hawk at all, but a small falcon. When hunting it hovers over one spot on winnowing wings, dropping suddenly to make a kill, usually a small mouse or vole.

other conditions to which they are adapted, and secondly the chances are that these resources will be used by a native species already adapted to the local environment by thousands or millions of years of evolution and therefore able to overwhelm the invaders in competing for food and other resources.

For these reasons, every part of the earth where there is terrestrial life at all has its own distinctive avifauna, yet with elements which it shares with many other parts of the world. Just as we find differences and strong resemblances between people in different places, so the traveller who notices birds finds a fascinating mixture of the familiar and the unfamiliar wherever he goes. In general the farther abroad he goes, the fewer familiar species he will see, but he will nearly always find members of bird families which he knows. Even in an Antarctic penguin colony he will probably find a member of the gull family, the Great Skua, stealing penguin eggs and chicks. This fierce predatory 'sea-hawk' has been seen closer to the South Pole than any other bird and is unique in having breeding populations in both polar regions.

SEA BIRDS

A traveller crossing the North Atlantic by ship will find that he does not leave all birds behind as the land disappears. Many birds get all their food from the sea and fly unimpeded from one productive area to another, provided no land mass intervenes. Therefore the transition is almost imperceptible as far as sea birds are concerned. Of course migrations will make the picture change with the seasons. In summer

one is likely to see some birds which nest in the southern hemisphere and are wintering in northern latitudes. The most conspicuous of them is the Greater Shearwater, somewhat smaller than a Herring Gull but with very long wings, whose rapid but graceful glide-flap-glide is a joy to watch. This bird nests in millions on the tiny volcanic islands of Tristan da Cunha and makes a great clockwise looping migration north as far as Greenland and Iceland.

Another southern sea bird whose migration loops into the North Atlantic is Wilson's Petrel. This little blackish bird with a white rump patch is so small that it is easy to overlook, but it is one of the most abundant birds in the world, possibly even the most abundant. It nests around the Antarctic Continent, but it reaches North American offshore waters in large numbers, feeding on surface plankton and small scraps dropped by the ships which it follows. These birds have a relative which remains in the northern hemisphere and may be seen in the North Atlantic at any season. This is the Fulmar, an opportunistic scavenger as well as a fisherman, which has been becoming abundant as a breeding species on cliffs around the British Isles, but whose breeding range on the western side of the Atlantic is still limited to arctic regions.

As a voyager approaches North America and enters the waters over the continental shelf, certain birds may appear which are not common in mid-Atlantic, but are found in offshore waters on both sides of the ocean. A chunky black and white diving bird with whirring flight on rather small wings will be a Puffin or another member of the auk family,

There are only six species of New World vultures, three of which occur in North America: the huge and now very rare Californian Condor, the fairly common Black Vulture (smallest member of the family) and the Turkey Vulture, pictured above, which is the best-known of all, widely distributed from Canada almost to the extreme south of South America.

The Spruce Grouse is a medium-sized game bird common in many evergreen woods from the United States-Canadian border northwards. It is specially remarkable for its fearlessness and indifference to man, in spite of the fact that it is hunted, a characteristic which has earned it the Canadian description of 'Fool Hen'.

the Alcidae. These are the northern counterparts of the penguins of the southern hemisphere, whose way of life, 'flying under water' to catch fish, is very similar. The living species of auks can all fly in the air, too, however, and are more closely related to the gulls and sandpipers than to the penguins. Their resemblance to penguins is due to convergent evolution in a similar environment. All the Atlantic members of this family are found on both sides of the ocean and would provide no 'new birds' for many European visitors, since most of them nest in more accessible places in the British Isles than in America. In the Pacific, however, there are several species of auks, especially small ones, not found in the Atlantic. The most spectacular North Atlantic sea bird, the Gannet, is also likely to appear over the continental shelf. This big white bird with black wingtips soars majestically over the ocean and feeds by plunging vertically from as high as a hundred feet above the surface. It has no external nostrils and uses its subcutaneous air sacs to cushion its body against the impact.

BIRDS OF COASTAL WATERS

The bird life begins to attain a distinctly American character only when we are in sight of land, but even here most of the birds will be familiar to a European. The characteristic birds of inshore waters are the gulls and terns, the cormorants, and, especially in winter, the loons or divers, the grebes, and the diving ducks. The terns, with their long pointed wings and forked tails, get their food in open water and migrate very long distances. These are probably the reasons why the

23

tern species of Europe and eastern North America are mostly the same. The Arctic Tern even includes an eastward crossing of the North Atlantic in its regular autumn migration to its Antarctic wintering grounds.

The gulls differ from the terns in being more generalized birds, feeding to a great extent from the ground. They scavenge along the shore; they go inland to eat berries and to catch worms and grubs in ploughed fields; one American species, Franklin's Gull, has an entirely inland breeding range. The Herring Gull and the Great Black-backed Gull and the very pelagic Kittiwake are common on both sides of the Atlantic, but several species of gull are found only on one side or the other.

The cormorants are large black diving birds which sit very low in the water, sometimes with little more than their heads and long necks exposed. Each side of the Atlantic has the Cormorant and one smaller species, but the relationships between the two species differ. In Europe the Shag is found in the same areas as the Cormorant, but feeding on fish of open water and very little on the bottom, where the Cormorant feeds. In North America, on the other hand, the Double-crested Cormorant, although apparently closely related to the Shag, scarcely overlaps the Cormorant at all geographically, but eats quite similar food. Furthermore, both species are more migratory than the European cormorants; in New England the Cormorant is the 'winter cormorant', while the Double-crested is the breeding species.

The other diving birds seen in winter on the coastal waters of New

Several kinds of nightjars occur in North America (mainly south of the Canadian border) of which the best known is probably this Nighthawk. This photograph shows the camouflage plumage very well and also a part of the conspicuous white wing band which is the best way of identifying this species. Nighthawks hunt for moths and other flying insects mostly during the twilight of dusk and dawn.

The Willet is a common bird of North America usually found along the shore. It is a large sandpiper appearing conspicuously grey when at rest, but in flight the bold black and white pattern in the wings is distinctive. This bird perched on a post is calling and probably has a young family nearby.

One of the four kinds of avocets is found only in America. As this striking photograph shows, it has the characteristic upswept bill, long legs and bold black and white markings, but a feature in this particular species is the brown head and neck.

England, the loons or divers, the grebes, and the diving ducks such as the scoters, goldeneyes, Common Eider, Scaup, Old-squaw or Long-tailed Ducks, and Red-breasted Merganser, are about the same as those of British coastal waters in winter. In sheltered coves and estuaries one will find a charming American duck, the Bufflehead, which looks like a miniature goldeneye with a big white patch on the head of the male. The Black Duck, which is not a diving duck, is common in winter on salt water just as the Mallard is in Europe.

The Wood Duck, also known as the Carolina, breeds throughout the United States and in the southernmost parts of Canada. The drake in spring presents a magnificent medley of colours and is perhaps as brightly plumaged as any duck in the world.

SHORE BIRDS

In summer nearly all the ducks are nesting inland or farther north, and the chief interest for the bird-watcher along the coast of eastern North America is usually the sandpipers and plovers of the beaches, especially in the late summer, when hordes of these birds are heading south after their short nesting season in the Arctic. These birds fly strongly with long pointed wings and often cross large expanses of ocean. Some of them do so regularly on their migrations, while others do it accidentally, driven off course by winds, and turn up unexpectedly as vagrants. Many of the species are different on the two sides of the Atlantic, yet most of the American species will look very much like a familiar species to the European. One large sandpiper which looks like nothing in Europe is the Willet, a rather nondescript light grey bird when at rest, which flashes a striking pattern of black and white when it spreads its wings. The Willet suffered severely when shooting these birds was legal, with the result that its breeding range is now interrupted. It nests in southern Nova Scotia and from southern New Jersey to the Gulf of Mexico, but in New England is not even seen as a migrant. The western population of Willets nests inland in the Great Plains, but its members winter on both the Atlantic and Pacific coasts.

One of the most remarkable birds to be seen along American beaches

America is rich in herons. This Louisiana Heron, on guard at its nest, is an elegant, medium-sized member of the group, dark blue above and white below, with long, thin green legs. It is common in the southern United States, but rarer in the north.

is a relative of the terns which lives in south-eastern U.S.A. and in South America, with close relatives in Africa and south-east Asia. This bird, the Black Skimmer, flies just over the surface of still water with its long knife-like lower jaw slicing through it. When it strikes a fish, the head is snapped down and the prey grabbed. The Skimmer's ability to do this with just a momentary slowing-down in flight is a dramatic illustration of the speed of birds' reflexes.

INLAND WATERS

For a number of reasons water birds show a stronger tendency to become widely distributed than land birds do. Even when we go inland to marshes, swamps, and lakes in North America, we find that the bird life has much in common with that of Europe. Mallard, teal, Pintail, and Shoveler can be found almost everywhere in the north temperate zone where there is suitable shallow water for ducks that tip up to feed. In much of eastern Canada and the United States, however, the Shoveler is absent, the other three are uncommon or absent as breeding species, and the commonest duck is the Black Duck, which looks like a very dark female Mallard. It interbreeds rather freely with the Mallard, and recent research suggests that it should perhaps be regarded as a dark race of the Mallard, better adapted than the green-headed form to a heavily-forested region with many small ponds and marshes. Now that much of the forest has been cleared, the typical Mallard is increasing in this region. Also to be seen in this part of North America is one of the most beautiful of ducks, the Wood or Carolina Duck. This bird became quite scarce in the early 20th century, but has made a good come-back, assisted by restrictions on shooting and by the erection of nest boxes over quiet streams and ponds, replacing the large hollow trees which have been cut away to a great extent.

The most majestic avian spectacle of America's lakes and rivers is probably the national bird of the United States, the Bald Eagle, soaring in the sunlight, and the most exciting spectacle is perhaps when a Bald Eagle chases an Osprey in an aerial 'dog-fight' until the fisherman drops its prey, and the eagle plunges down to retrieve it. This magnificent bird occurs throughout the United States and Canada, but is becoming scarce except in Alaska. The reasons for this dwindling are not fully known, but DDT poisoning is a prominent suspect.

The large wading birds of American ponds and marshes, like the ducks, run the gamut from species identical with those of Europe, like the Black-crowned Night Heron, through doubtfully distinct species, like the American Great Blue Heron and the European Grey Heron, to species with no counterpart in Europe, like the little Green Heron. To see these birds at their best, one needs to go to the Everglades of Florida or to the large heronries of Louisiana and elsewhere on the Gulf Coast, where not only these, but other herons, Wood Storks, ibises, and Roseate Spoonbills may be seen. Many of these birds, especially the egrets, were nearly wiped out by plume hunters in the 19th century, but protection, largely brought about by the National Audubon Society, has enabled them to recover magnificently in this century. The most spectacular increase in numbers by any bird in America, however, has been that of the Cattle Egret. This African bird reached

South America about eighty years ago, apparently unaided by man. It was not mentioned in books of North American birds as recently as the 1940s, but now it is the commonest heron in many places in Florida; it has been reported from throughout the eastern states, and has nested as far north as Ontario. It follows cattle or even rides on them, picking up insects disturbed by the grazing beasts. This 'ecological niche' or place in the biological community was not previously occupied by a comparable native American bird; so there was no competition to hinder this remarkably successful invasion.

LAND BIRDS

When we turn our attention to North America's land birds, we find a fauna in which groups of birds which evolved in Central and South America meet elements from Europe and Asia. Our knowledge of the origins of bird families is far from complete, but it appears that many South American families expanded into North America, taking advantage of its great area and long summer days in high latitudes, affording ample time for food-gathering. Apparently the only one of about seventy families now found in North America whose initial separation from its relatives actually occurred on this continent is the turkey family, with only two species. Many individual species originated in North America, however. This is especially true of the passerine birds or perching birds, the order to which more than half of all birds and all the small 'song birds' belong. A South American would recognize many species of North American passerine birds as winter

ABOVE The Yellow-crowned Night Heron, ranging from the United States to central South America, is a dumpy heron, with a distinctive black-and-white head pattern and a small white crest which has a touch of yellow at the crown. The five large eggs look rather unsafe in the fragile nest built of sticks, especially when the bird adds her own weight in settling to brood them.

TOP RIGHT The American Robin is a large thrush with a distinctive reddish brown breast. It nests far up into Canada, but is a summer migrant wintering in the southern United States and Central America.

RIGHT The handsome Blue Jay is like the Jay of Europe a member of the crow family. It is amongst the commonest birds of southern Canada and throughout the whole of the United States.

28

visitors to his continent, but only twenty-five of the 175 species of passerine birds regularly found in eastern North America are also found in Europe. Four of these are European birds which were introduced by man in the 19th century, four are birds which nest mainly in arctic or alpine tundra, eleven nest mainly in the coniferous woods of the north and the mountains, and only six species have rather wide distributions south of these regions. These six are the Horned Lark (Shore Lark), Barn Swallow (Swallow), Bank Swallow (Sand Martin), Magpie, Black-capped Chickadee (Willow Tit), and Northern Shrike (Great Grey Shrike).

CITIES AND SUBURBS

The introduced Starling, House Sparrow, and Rock Dove are abundant in the cities of eastern North America, just as recent human immigrants are. These rather aggressive and not too specialized birds have been introduced in various places in North America and elsewhere; not finding effective established competitors, they have prospered. In American suburbs one continues to find these immigrants, but one finds old Americans, too.

Suburban gardens and shady trees provide food, nest sites, and general habitats for a wide variety of song birds and other small birds in summer in America, as they do in most places. The climate, which is dominated by a continent instead of an ocean, is hot in summer and cold in winter, especially inland, encouraging the evolution of migratory habits, and resulting in few birds at certain seasons. Of course, there are certain visitors from farther north at suburban feeding tables in winter. One of the commonest of these is the Tree Sparrow, a trim bunting with a reddish-brown cap, streaked back, and a spot in the middle of its cheeks, which breeds in the stunted trees of northern Canada. Among the residents which stay throughout the year are the Downy Woodpecker and its larger edition, the Hairy Woodpecker, the colourful and noisy Blue Jay, and the Black-capped Chickadee. Farther south the year-round residents of the suburbs include the Mockingbird, the best mimic in an American family of mimics.

The Cardinal, a large crested finch, bright red from beak to tail, used to be regarded as a southern bird, too, but it has been steadily expanding its range northward in recent years and is now common as far north as Massachusetts. The Cardinal's plumage adds a note of tropical gaiety to northern winters, but in summer it has several rivals in feathered splendour. Swinging from the tips of the branches of elms in towns and villages from Nova Scotia to Alberta and from Georgia to Texas are the pouch-like woven nests of the Baltimore Oriole, whose loud whistled song calls attention to the male just in case one might overlook his flaming orange and black plumage. This bird superficially resembles the Golden Oriole of the Old World, but it belongs to a large and varied family, the Icteridae, sometimes called American black-birds, whose members are found from Patagonia to Alaska and Labrador. Another New World family, with less variety of size and shape than the Icteridae, but more variety of dazzling tropical colours, is the tanager family, represented in the east by the all-red Summer Tanager and the red and black Scarlet Tanager and in the west by the yellow, red, and black Western Tanager.

Of all the birds of American gardens the most glamorous are the hummingbirds. These smallest of all birds have gleaming metallic plumage which flashes green, red, blue, purple and other colours, depending on the species, when it catches the sun as they hover over flowers, sipping nectar. Only one species is found in the east, but California is blessed with seven species and Arizona with twelve. Many more species occur in tropical America. Hummingbirds are found only in the Americas, but in the Old World tropics they are replaced by small, brilliantly-coloured nectar-eating birds, the sunbirds, flower-peckers, and honeyeaters, which are passerine birds.

WOODS

These birds of suburban gardens are also found around farms and certain kinds of woodlands. In the major agricultural areas of the Middle West and California, most of the land is cleared and cultivated, with occasional small patches of woodland beside streams, but in the east there are large areas of cleared land that are growing back to woods. The western mountains also have extensive brushy areas growing back to woods after being cut over for lumber. These brushy transitional areas and the edges of woods provide especially favourable habitats for many kinds of birds, due to their variety and to their relatively rapid growth, furnishing plenty of food, directly and by way of insects. One bird which thrives in such areas is the Chestnut-sided Warbler, which was rare in Audubon's time, in the early 19th century, but is now one of the commonest members of its family in

LEFT The Black-capped Chickadee, a small titmouse found in the northern United States and in Canada, is the same species as the Marsh Tit of Britain and Europe. It is a bird that is readily attracted to the garden feeding table, especially in hard weather.

BELOW Four hummingbirds breed in North America, mainly in the south and south-west, but the beautiful Ruby-throated is found on the eastern side as far north as southern Ontario and Quebec and in New Brunswick. They are so tiny that they only weigh about one-eighth of an ounce. The nest is only about an inch across; when feeding their young they thrust the whole of their long bills down the throat of the chick to pour partly digested food into its stomach.

southern Canada and north-eastern United States. Its family, the wood warblers or Parulidae, is one of the most distinctive, attractive, and interesting families of American birds. It is a different family from the Sylviidae, the warblers of the Old World. Both are groups of small, lively insectivorous birds which occupy similar ecological niches in many cases, but are strikingly different in appearance for the most part. The Old World warblers are largely dull-coloured and inconspicuous; several species with olive-brown backs and whitish underparts are almost indistinguishable in the field. The wood warblers, however, especially the males, show in their breeding plumage a variety of brilliant and distinctive colour patterns, with yellow and orange predominating, as in the Parula Warbler, the Magnolia Warbler, and the American Redstart (not to be confused with the European Redstart, a thrush). These patterns enable bird-watchers and undoubtedly the birds themselves to identify the species of the wearers, while in the Old World warblers the loud, vigorous songs make identification possible. The wood warblers have distinctive songs, too, but in general they are not as loud and musical.

Although several species of wood warblers may occupy the same habitat, they avoid competition by feeding in different ways and thus on different kinds of insects. Along with them we can often find members of another insectivorous American family, the vireos, resembling Old World warblers in being rather plain-coloured and having rich songs, but slightly larger and less active than most warblers. The Red-eyed Vireo, which sings all day long, is one of the commonest and audibly most distinctive birds of the North American deciduous woodlands. The most conspicuous bird of these woodlands from a visual standpoint has now completely vanished. The Passenger Pigeon, a medium-sized, highly gregarious pigeon, was slaughtered by the million, and is now extinct.

FIELDS AND PRAIRIES

Extensive treeless fields are less favourable to bird life than mixed or brushy areas, but some birds are adapted to feeding in or over them and some to nesting in them. Those which obtain food in open areas but nest in trees are likely to be seen perching on wires along roads. The handsome little American Kestrel or Sparrowhawk does this. So do the kingbirds; these are members of a large American passerine family, the tyrant flycatchers, which resemble the Old World flycatchers in sitting upright on exposed branches from which they sally forth to snap up insects with their broad, flattened bills. The names 'tyrant' and 'kingbird' refer to the habit of several of the larger species of pugnaciously driving off large birds, such as hawks and crows. Most of the tyrant flycatchers are rather plain-coloured, even the hundreds of species in the tropics, but the Vermilion Flycatcher, at least the male, is as gaudy as it sounds, and the Scissor-tailed Flycatcher of the southern Midwest is a very striking pale grey bird with salmon-pink sides and wing linings and an extremely long forked tail.

In open places in the southern states one can almost always see a Turkey Vulture, commonly called 'buzzard', soaring overhead looking for dead animals. Its relative, the California Condor, is one of North America's largest, shyest and rarest birds.

AFRICAN BIRDS

ABOVE These Greater Flamingos have been joined by these Grey Gulls and African Skimmers. Skimmers, which are found also in America, are extremely graceful birds, related to the gulls and unique amongst birds because their lower mandibles are much longer than the upper ones.

RIGHT The male of the Paradise Flycatcher is characterized by its long, central tail feathers.

LEFT Adult flamingos looking for food on Lake Magadi, Kenya.

Ostriches are the biggest living birds, full-grown adults standing over five feet in height and weighing anything up to around three hundredweight! Once numerous and widespread in Africa, they are now usually found only in wildlife reserves. Like their relations the rheas, Emus and Cassowaries, Ostriches are flightless but they can travel at speeds of twenty to thirty miles per hour on their long legs, which are so powerful that an aggressive bird can kick a man unconscious with one blow.

Pelicans of Lake Naivasha in Kenya

Cormorants, Spoonbills, Snakebirds and
Ibises on the same lake

The toucan, indigenous to Central and South America

The House Sparrows which often become such unwelcome pests in Europe and America are related to the weaver birds of Africa and originated in that continent. Whilst some weaver birds build nests as untidy as those of the House Sparrow, many build very neat nests. Most are communal in their nesting-sites, like these Social Weavers which have built their enormous nests in a camel-thorn on the South African veld. Each 'block of flats' will accommodate hundreds of nests and with quarters so close it is not perhaps surprising that polygamy is a commonplace.

A pair of Fiscal Shrikes in Kenya use a bunch of bananas as a nesting place.

ABOVE Snakes and lizards are numerous in Africa and are often taken by birds-of-prey. This Black-breasted Snake Eagle in Rhodesia has captured a cobra with which to feed its young.

LEFT Africa is especially rich in birds-of-prey, including vultures, which perform useful work as scavengers and are generally tolerated. These big Hooded Vultures are feeding on the head of a wildebeest in the Gorongozo game reserve, East Africa.

RIGHT In South Africa vultures are deliberately poisoned by farmers, even though they do no damage. This Cape Vulture is alighting at its nest on a cliff-edge at Bredasdorp, Cape Province – the southernmost breeding-colony of this species.

AUSTRALIAN AND NEW ZEALAND BIRDS

RIGHT Just as the Kiwi is associated with New Zealand, so the Kookaburra is with Australia, where it is a common species. A large member of the kingsfisher family, the Kookaburra has a number of loud, shrieking cries by which it has earned the popular nickname of 'laughing jackass'.

BELOW RIGHT There are over a score of different bee-eaters, all in the Old World. Most are beautifully coloured and have highly elongated, central tail-feathers. They are graceful in flight, yet may have a curious jinking action, as if they were aerial puppets operated by strings. The Australian species, caught in the act of seizing a wild bee, is a summer migrant, moving north to tropical climates during the southern winter.

LEFT The handsome Black Swan of Australia possibly rivals both the Emu and the Kookaburra as a national emblem. It has been introduced as an ornamental bird to many parts of the world, including New Zealand, where many are now breeding successfully in a wild state.

The avocets are amongst the most elegant of all birds. There are only four kinds in the world, and of these the one found in Australia is probably the second rarest. This bird is just arranging her eggs with the typical delicate, upswept bill before settling to incubate them.

The Plain Turkey is one of the largest bustards in the world and is found only in Australia. It is often known locally simply as the 'wild turkey', but bustards are not closely related to the true turkey.

RIGHT Many kinds of duck inhabit Australia but this beautiful Pink-eared Duck, sitting on its nest in a tree, is found only in that country.

LEFT Frogmouths are very curious birds, closely related to the nightjars but more owl-like in their habits. This big Tawny Frogmouth of Australia shows the hooked beak and the cryptically-patterned plumage which makes it difficult to spot a bird when it is motionless or sleeping.

LEFT Two of the smallest penguins are found in Australia and New Zealand. The Yellow-eyed Penguin is found only in New Zealand and stands only one-and-a-half feet in height. Unlike most members of its family, it nests in burrows or recesses in rocks as do the . . .

BELOW . . . Fairy Penguins, found in south Australia and Tasmania as well as in New Zealand. These tiny penguins are even smaller than the Yellow-eyed and are, in fact, the smallest in the world.

RIGHT The Tui is a common New Zealand bird which is named after its call.

BELOW Another curious and primitive bird, the Kiwi, is found only in New Zealand. They are only a quarter of the size of the Emu, with short, stout legs and long, slightly decurved bills with which they dig in mud for worms and other food. They are inconspicuous birds, living in swamps and nesting in holes but they are firmly entrenched as New Zealand's national symbol.

The flightless Emu, a primitive bird, is found only in Australia and the wild population is being steadily reduced by the spread of civilization. The Emu has few natural enemies and can usually make a speedy retreat from danger on its strong, thick legs but . . .

. . . escape may not be so easy in the breeding season. The eggs are laid in August, usually ten to twelve in number. They are large and must present quite a problem to the male as he settles to brood them. Once having laid the eggs, the female leaves all the domestic duties to her mate.

The eggs hatch after about two months of incubation. The plumage of the chick is a bold pattern of black and white and they are very active within a week or two after hatching, foraging for themselves though the male remains in attendance.

LEFT The White-bellied Sea Eagle is one of the grandest birds in a group which includes the White-tailed Sea Eagle of northern Europe and the Bald Eagle of America. This bird is about to alight at its tree-eyrie in Malaya.

LEFT This White Ibis is found in southern Asia and is closely related to the Sacred Ibis of Africa, which appears so frequently in Egyptian history. Ibises all have strong, down-curved bills and long legs, and are generally found in marshy places almost throughout the tropical and subtropical regions of the world.

BELOW The Ibisbill is a member of the small family of stilts and avocets, but is unlike them in not generally frequenting lowland marshes, for it breeds high in the Himalayan Mountains. This photograph was taken in Sikkim.

ASIAN BIRDS

The Openbill Stork with young, showing the extraordinary development of the mandibles.

RIGHT Darters nesting at Bharatpur, India. Darters, like cormorants, which they so closely resemble in appearance and habits, usually nest in colonies and are found in tropical and subtropical regions of both the Old and New World.

In China and Japan cormorants have been used for centuries in fishing.

Cuckoo-shrikes are neither shrikes nor cuckoos. There are many kinds, almost all inhabitants of tropical rain forests. This Giant Cuckoo-shrike is about to feed its young with a lizard.

BIRD MIGRATION
KENNETH WILLIAMSON

Migration movements are often especially impressive because of the sheer numbers which may be involved. Adverse weather conditions may hold up movement for many days; then, when the weather changes, the birds surge forth like water long pent-up by floodgates. Here in America a part of a great concourse of Snow and White-fronted Geese are on the move again after a short rest. These breed in the Arctic and winter in the southern part of the United States. The Mississippi valley is a renowned flyway for geese.

True migration is the regular seasonal movement of groups of animals, whether they be insects, fishes, birds, seals, whales or other mammals. Its purpose is to secure for the participants the best environmental conditions at all times of the year. Migratory behaviour has been most closely studied in relation to birds, especially those of the northern hemisphere whose year is divided between vast areas of tundra and forest, which sustain life on a generous scale in the summer months, and tropical or warm-temperate regions which afford a winter haven when the north is frozen and inhospitable. Many such birds undertake journeys of prodigious length, but shorter ones are accomplished even within the tropics, usually to exploit new food resources induced by seasonal rains. At sea, the lives of many species oscillate between parts of the ocean affording a rich plankton fauna — usually the cold currents and the neighbourhood of polar ice — and a restricted land area suitable for breeding.

Migration among birds is primarily a means of securing the best available food supply at a given time, and there is general agreement that the behaviour originated to meet this end. This does not necessarily mean that it remains the primary factor stimulating each fresh outburst of activity, and indeed it is a commonplace observation that most birds begin their travels long before the local food shortage becomes acute. The behaviour has become an integral part of the seasonal cycle of the bird's life, taking its turn in proper sequence with courtship, nest-building, the rearing of young, and the moult. Like these, it can be performed only when certain physiological changes

53

Birds on migration, especially the larger species like the eagles, buzzards, cranes and geese, provide some of the most beautiful spectacles in all nature. These Sandhill Cranes, with a wing-spread of nearly six feet, were photographed in the autumn moving south across Alaska from northern breeding-grounds to spend the winter in the southern United States and Central America.

(among them the deposition of increased body-fat to act as a fuel reserve for the long journey) have prepared the bird for the experience. Stimuli derived from the external environment play their part, but the exact nature of these stimuli is still not fully understood. Reduction of available feeding time by the shortening days of autumn, changes in temperature (rising in spring, falling in autumn), changes in barometric pressure (especially the development of anticyclones or 'highs') and perhaps other factors, separately or cumulatively, affect the bird once it is ready to depart.

A number of techniques have been developed for studying this fascinating subject. The most important, since it is the basis of most of our factual knowledge, is bird-ringing, or 'banding' as it is known in America. Today most civilized countries have their banding scheme, under which trained personnel are issued with light metal rings (usually of monel or an aluminium alloy) to put on the legs of birds. Each ring has a serial number and the address of the headquarters. The data of 'recovery' can be matched with the appropriate banding record whenever a ring is found and reported, and in this way a great deal has been learned about the directions taken by migrants, the location of their winter quarters, their speed of movement, the hazards to which they are exposed, and so on, all over the world.

The oldest banding schemes have been in existence half a century or so, while co-ordinated schemes for the reporting and analysis of observations on migration in progress have a much shorter history. Several European countries, Sweden, East and West Germany,

Following pages

Pyrrhuloxia in flight

Blue Jay

Japanese Blue Flycatcher

Holland, Switzerland, and also the Estonian S.S.R. have such organizations, while in Britain a network of twenty or more permanently manned 'bird observatories' has grown up since the war, mostly on islands and headlands round the coast, where much valuable research has been done into the effects of winds and weather on migrating birds. The majority of these observatories have a standard recording system and a central clearing-house in the British Trust for Ornithology; they also maintain large wire-netting traps in which several thousand birds are caught annually for examination and ringing.

Along the eastern seaboard of the United States a similar chain of observation stations combines in 'Operation Recovery', the aim being to capture, band and recapture migrants, using batteries of barely-visible silk or nylon 'mist-nets' which were introduced from Japan shortly after the war. Their effectiveness in trapping free-flying migrants wherever the birds tend to concentrate has greatly accelerated ringing and recovery rates, and has revolutionized bird study in America and Europe. In recent years a powerful new tool has been found in radar, for migrating birds cast echoes on a radar screen, so that their course can be plotted and filmed, and the record analysed at leisure. Radar studies in Switzerland, Great Britain and the United States have taught us much concerning the volume of migration at different seasons and under varying weather conditions, and about the track and heading of flocks in relation to the wind. It has shown that whilst most migration takes place at heights below five thousand feet, some birds — the waders especially — frequently travel at ten thousand or twelve thousand feet. A further contribution has come from teams of American workers who plotted movements from calculations made after observing through telescopes the passage of birds across the face of the full moon.

Migration is manifested in markedly different ways, even among closely related birds. Among North American wood-warblers the wholly insectivorous ones spend the winter in tropical America, but the Myrtle Warbler of the coniferous forests has a more varied diet including berries and seeds, and moves a much shorter distance to the south-eastern states and Mexico. 'Operation Recovery' has shown that a few, like the Blackpoll Warbler, after resting near the coast and suddenly increasing their weight, cross the ocean to Bermuda and the West Indies, and fly on to Guyana and Brazil. Among Old World leaf warblers the Arctic Warbler journeys from Lapland across Siberia before turning southwards through China to the islands of Indonesia, while the east Siberian race of the Willow Warbler takes a virtually opposite route from the Kolyma River region to the Kenya highlands. Individuals of these small birds, weighing only a third of an ounce, may cover between seven and eight thousand miles twice a year. By contrast, many Himalayan leaf warblers migrate altitudinally, finding their seasonal habitats at different levels among the foothills and steep mountain-sides.

Wild geese travel in tribal flocks and stay together throughout the winter, returning together to their nesting-grounds in Greenland, Spitzbergen and northern Europe; or, in America, travelling along well-known 'flyways' which usually follow the major river valleys — such as the Mississippi north to the Great Lakes, and on down the

Kingfisher

Mackenzie to the barrenlands of the Canadian Arctic. When the Icelandic Whooper Swans reach Scotland in October they stay on the lochs in discrete family parties, for the cygnets need the leadership and experience of their elders. No such bond exists among the ducks; with them pairing takes place in winter quarters, and this often gives rise to a peculiar movement called 'abmigration', when local birds pair with visiting drakes from far afield and travel hundreds of miles from their native heath to breed. In this way Scottish Teal have been discovered nesting in Poland and Russia.

Although the geese and swans show their young the way this is the exception rather than the rule. There are species, like the Gannet, in which the young begin their first migration by swimming solitarily out to sea; the migration habit is strong in the first two or three years, as in a number of sea-birds, but then declines so that the adult is merely a wanderer. The young Cuckoo, which never knows its real parents, must find the way to Africa entirely on its own, and the same is true of the parasitic cowbirds for their journey from North to South America.

Two New Zealand cuckoos have an even more miraculous migration: the Bronze Cuckoo crosses the South Pacific to the Solomon Islands, where it stays from May to September, and the Long-tailed Cuckoo spends a similar period scattered over a vast segment of Oceania, but chiefly in the Fiji, Samoa, Tonga, Ellice and Society Islands. Both cross ocean gaps of between two and three thousand miles wide in preference to taking a safer route *via* eastern Australia

Manx Shearwaters only come to land to breed and nest in burrows in the cliffs. Male and female take turns at the nest, each spell occupying several days. The duty bird has to live on its fat whilst its mate may be several hundred miles away fishing and feeding and putting on enough weight to enable it, too, to withstand a foodless week.

The Arctic Tern may well be the world's greatest avian traveller. Birds which breed near the Arctic Circle migrate to the Southern Pacific. Terns which breed in North America cross the Atlantic into European waters before moving south with Old World nesters. Many birds must complete journeys of seven or eight thousand miles twice a year.

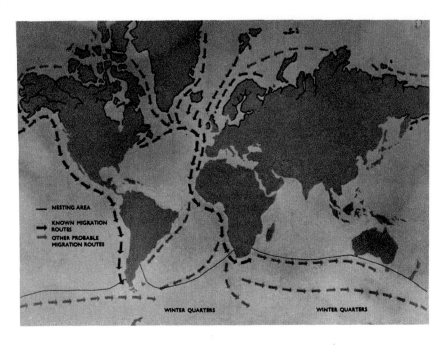

Migration of the Arctic Tern.

and New Guinea, but at the time of their departure from New Zealand the prevailing winds are from the south-east and undoubtedly helpful. The Wheatears of Greenland and the east Canadian Arctic have nearly as long and hazardous a sea-crossing, for in common with Snow and Lapland Buntings and the even smaller Arctic Redpolls, they fly non-stop to the British Isles by 'cyclonic approach' in the backing westerly winds of North Atlantic depressions.

Sea-birds are not less migratory than land-birds. Millions of Great Shearwaters nest under the soil of the Tristan da Cunha islands from October till March, and afterwards wander in a great circle over the Atlantic, crossing from American to European seas via Labrador, Greenland and the British Isles, and homing from the bulge of West Africa. The Short-tailed Shearwater of South Australia and Tasmania has an equally fantastic migration, describing a huge figure-of-eight over the Pacific. When breeding finishes in May the flocks head north-east till well beyond New Zealand, then swing north-west towards Japan (which they reach after about a month), circle northwards past Kamchatka, the Aleutian Islands and Alaska to skirt western North America, before striking across the full width of the ocean to northern Australia, whence they finally coast south to begin a new nesting season in Bass Strait. The peculiar double loop thus made is correlated with the prevailing winds which assist the birds on their way. Similar loop migrations of the Sooty Shearwater and the much smaller Wilson's Petrel, which nest in Antarctica, are also a response to the prevailing winds.

Knots are small wading-birds which nest in the high Arctic, moving south each autumn in vast numbers. This huge gathering was photographed in October in the estuary of the Cheshire Dee, in north-west England.

BOTTOM LEFT Some birds migrate by day, like the Swift, which is able to feed on the wing as it lives on small flies. Many small birds, however, migrate at night, an arrangement which enables them to spend the day in feeding and resting to restore their strength for the next stage of the hazardous journey. Many birds which undertake long journeys over the sea weigh an ounce or less and may well lose a quarter of their body-weight in the effort.

RIGHT The Swallow breeds widely in all the temperate zones of the northern hemisphere and also travels by day. Ringing has shown that birds from central Europe winter in tropical Africa, whilst British breeding-birds usually fly farther south, even to the Cape Province and Natal.

Many Shearwaters of the British Isles migrate south-west across the equator and there have now been a number of recoveries of ringed birds off the coast of Brazil five thousand miles from home. Some may go even farther, for a bird ringed at Skokholm off the Welsh coast on 9th September 1960 was found washed up on the beach at Venus Bay in South Australia on 22nd November 1961. It may have gone too far to the south, as has happened occasionally with Common and Arctic Terns, specimens of which have turned up at Fremantle in Western Australia nearly nine thousand miles from their birthplace in northern Europe. Such vagrants are probably blown round the Cape of Good Hope and across the Indian Ocean in the westerly wind belt. This belt, the Roaring Forties, is responsible for the unique migrations of the Giant Petrel and certain albatrosses bred on Antarctic isles: these large sea-birds have a long period of immaturity (reckoned to be six or seven years) during which they soar round and round the world on the westerly wind in these latitudes. A young Wandering Albatross which probably left the nest on Kerguelen Island in early December of 1952 was found dead at Parache, Chile, on 1st October 1953, having travelled well over eight thousand miles; a ringed Royal Albatross journeyed from Campbell Island, south of New Zealand, to Santiago Province in Chile inside six months.

The most travelled bird in the world may well be the Arctic Tern: the bulk of this species nest within the Arctic Circle, and many penetrate the South Polar pack-ice in the winter time. Birds from eastern Canada, New England and Greenland first cross the Atlantic to the European side, keeping to the colder waters where food is abundant, and then strike southwards to Africa, sometimes rounding the Cape to enter the Indian Ocean. One ringed in west Greenland in July was found at Durban, Natal, after travelling more than eleven thousand miles in only three months, an average of at least 120 miles per day; another took fifteen weeks to fly the nine thousand miles from Turnevik Bay, Labrador, to Port Shepstone, Natal.

The returns from bird-ringing show that different species, and sometimes different populations within a species, have a different route-preference or 'standard direction' between their summer and winter homes. The majority of European song-birds, including the Common Whitethroat and most other warblers, move south-west into France and Iberia en route for Africa; but the Lesser Whitethroat and Wood Warbler take a south-east route, and while recoveries of the former in Lebanon and Israel show that the species reaches Africa round the eastern Mediterranean, recoveries of the latter in Italy indicate that it makes a short sea-crossing via Sicily and Tunis. Most of the European Blackcaps and Spotted Flycatchers travel south-east, but about longitude 10—11 degrees east there is a 'migratory divide' beyond which the populations (including the British stocks) have a standard direction to the south-west.

Some American birds have different routes for the spring and fall, the best-known example being the American Golden Plover which nests on the barrenlands of Canada. They go east to Labrador after breeding, then make a three thousand mile hop across the ocean to Brazil, returning by a mainly overland route in spring through Central America and the Gulf States. The western form of this same species

The beautiful Bluethroat, a migrant which winters in the tropics but breeds in northern Eurasia, has crossed the Bering Sea to nest in north-western America. But it still recrosses the sea in autumn to follow the traditional flyways to its winter-quarters.

This Lesser Whitethroat is an Old World warbler distinguished from the Common Whitethroat by dark feathers over the ears. Both of these small warblers are summer migrants, breeding in northern Europe, and both winter in Africa. But ringing has shown that, whereas the Common Whitethroat flies directly south through France and Spain, the Lesser Whitethroat moves south-east through the Balkan countries and round the eastern Mediterranean into Africa.

crosses the wide wastes of the Pacific from Alaska to the Hawaiian Islands and beyond. It is not the only American wader to do so, for the Bristle-thighed Curlew (whose Alaskan breeding-grounds were discovered only a decade ago), the Wandering Tattler and Bauer's Godwit also spend the off-season in these and other Pacific Islands, some flying as far as New Zealand. Some Siberian waders, such as the Knot, frequently reach the Antipodes.

Occasionally a bird's migration retraces the route of a relatively recent invasion into a new area. The expanding range of the Wheatear provides the best example of 'back-track' migration of this kind. On the one side of the world it has spread from Greenland into the Canadian Arctic, but moves back across the Atlantic in the westerlies of the storm-track before making its way through Britain, France and Spain to West Africa. On the other side of the world it has penetrated from Siberia through Alaska to far eastern Canada, and these birds return across the Bering Strait and the whole of Asia to East Africa.

Some populations have what is called a 'leap-frog migration', with those breeding farthest north wintering farthest south; thus the tundra race of the Ringed Plover and the Redshank of northern Europe overshoot the summer and winter ranges of their temperate zone representatives to winter in tropical Africa and the Mediterranean basin respectively. Some species are 'partial migrants' only, those birds breeding furthest north moving south in autumn, joining the resident groups of milder or more temperate regions. The American Robin and its cousin the European Blackbird belong to this group,

and in some of these species we find that the males are less disposed to move than the females while the young are more migratory than either.

One of the truly remarkable features of this twice yearly coming and going of vast multitudes of birds is that so many make their journeys during the hours of darkness, in order to reserve the daylight for finding food and replenishing lost strength. The drain on their resources may be severe: studies at Fair Isle Bird Observatory in Shetland have shown that a loss in body-weight of up to 40 per cent may occur in Greenland Wheatears and Redpolls during a long-distance overseas flight, but that these and other small birds have a marvellous power of recuperation if they can stay 'off-passage' for a week or more in a suitable habitat. Generally speaking, insectivorous birds such as the thrushes, warblers and flycatchers migrate by night, whilst the seed-eating finches and buntings move by day.

The swifts and the related swallows, which can feed on aerial plankton as they go, and sometimes larks, pipits and wagtails are also day-migrants. So too are White Storks and many birds-of-prey, especially the broad-winged buzzards and eagles, for these require the rising air-currents beneath cumulus clouds to lift them to a great height, when they glide effortlessly on their way, gradually descending to the base of another thermal. Such conditions do not occur after sunset, nor do they occur over the sea, so that the best places to watch stork and bird-of-prey migrations are where great concentrations occur at short sea-crossings such as the Bosphorus and Straits of Gibraltar.

The accumulated evidence from banding and other sources indi-

The Yellow Wagtail is another small migrant which, like the Bluethroat, crosses from Asia to Alaska to nest. Both these species could doubtless winter well in central America, but the 'built-in' instinct to return whence they have come is far too strong for this to happen.

ABOVE Many cuckoos are great travellers. This European Cuckoo breeds freely as far north as Scotland and Scandinavia, migrating in autumn south-east rather than south, passing the winter in north-east Africa. The adult cuckoos, having left their domestic worries with foster-parents, move south in July, leaving the young birds to follow, quite unaided, in September.

ABOVE RIGHT The Blackbird of Europe has similar habits and is closely related to the American Robin and though not so attractively coloured it has a finer song, regarded by many as second-to-none.

cates that most birds have a highly developed faculty for accurate orientation — indeed, without such a faculty migratory stocks could not survive. Research by G.V.T. Matthews in England and the late Gustav Kramer in Germany has shown that day fliers are able to navigate by observation of the sun's position in the sky, while Sauer and his associates have shown that night migrants are able to find their way by some form of stellar navigation. This implies that birds must be equipped with some sensitive timing mechanism which takes note of the apparent motion of sun and stars across the sky, and the nature of this 'internal clock' is a mystery which students of navigation are still trying to probe. A prerequisite of successfully oriented flight is that the cloud amount must be small and must not obscure the heavenly bodies; if there is heavy cloud, fog, rain or drizzle the orintation mechanism breaks down. This much has been shown by experimental workers, and there is abundant evidence of it in the sometimes huge 'falls' of migrants which occur at the bird observatories with the passing of stormy wather.

The weather undoubtedly plays an important (perhaps the most important) part in the success or failure of a migratory journey. Analysis of the British bird observatories' data shows that movement is heavy during anticyclonic weather, and this may well be because the subsiding air of anticyclones tends to dissipate cloud, so permitting accurate orientation, while the light airs within a high pressure system reduce the risk of deflection by wind-drift from the chosen course. Movements may also take place in cold weather, which is often connected with anticyclonic weather. They may also occur after a 'hold up' due to the passing of depressions with their associated heavy cloud and rainfall, being triggered off by the cold polar air which sweeps in behind, raising the barometric pressure and clearing the skies. Nevertheless, anticyclones bring the ideal conditions, and when the continental highs cover vast areas of the northern lands in late summer, millions of birds which have attained a state of internal readiness get under way on the first stage of their adventurous journey.

The regular alternation of these movements distinguishes true migration from the periodic mass eruptions from the breeding area of certain mammals (such as the lemming), insects (such as the Monarch Butterfly of America), and some species of northern birds. Swarms of Desert Locusts travel downwind for thousands of miles seeking regions of atmospheric convergence which provide the rainfall essential for breeding, but in the majority of cases the spur to these irregular wanderings is serious overcrowding in the home area brought about by exceptionally favourable conditions for the rearing and survival of young. Unlike the regular migrants, which seek a known summer or winter home, the 'invasion species' are in quest of new food sources, which they exploit until exhaustion of the crop forces them to move on. The most striking examples in Europe and America are the sporadic excursions from the northern coniferous forests of Crossbills and Waxwings, but a number of other species, such as the Siskin in Europe and the Evening Grosbeak in the United States, show similar behaviour. Nothing definite is known of their navigational powers, and indeed it seems likely that the dispersal is a random one, though in Europe the prevailing anticyclonic airstreams invest it with a generally westwards flow. It is a feature of wanderings of this kind that a proportion of the birds are absorbed by new areas where life-conditions are suitable, so that colonization (sometimes only temporary) takes place, and there is seldom a return movement on anything like the same massive scale.

The gap between true migration and such irregular wandering is not as wide as once seemed the case, however, and indeed there may be no real gap at all. Dispersion on a wide scale is theoretically possibly in any species when circumstances combine to permit a big increase in numbers, and the appropriate behaviour is probably much the same whether the subject is a migratory one or not. Every autumn anticyclonic east winds bring large numbers of birds across the North Sea to Scotland, many belonging to species which should be oriented the other way, or at least giving the British Isles a wide berth in such perfect travelling weather. Similar conditions over France produce southerly winds which deposit south European migrants on the Channel coast of England and at the Irish Sea observatories. These falls include great rarities from distant parts of Eurasia, bred many hundreds of miles away, as well as extralimital species from the Mediterranean. In America, south-west winds often carry similarly exotic species from southern and mid-western states to New England banding stations. In Britain, certain species figure in unusual strength in certain years — indeed, the visitations have an 'invasion' quality, and what we witness is not real migration but a mass movement of dispersion kind, comprising mainly the surplus, pioneering element — the young birds of the year.

The American Robin, actually a thrush, is one of the few American birds which has occasionally successfully flown the Atlantic to be recorded in Europe. It is a migrant in Canada and the northern parts of its range, but birds nesting in the warmer south are resident, a state of affairs which is shared by a number of other birds.

The Common Tern only makes a shallow scrape in sand or pebbles in which to lay her two or three eggs. Occasionally a little dried seaweed may be gathered and placed around the nest but this is ornamental rather than functional.

The variety of birds' nests is enormous. While some birds make no proper nest at all, laying their eggs like the Guillemot on a bare rock ledge, others build the most elaborate nests such as those of the weaver birds of India and Africa. Nests may be in natural holes or crannies or in excavated holes as woodpeckers' in trees and Sand Martins' in sandy cliffs. They may be at the tops of tall trees or on the ground or in holes underground, floating on water or on the shore just above the tide line. Many sea birds only come to land to breed and the Emperor Penguin never comes to land at all, laying its single egg on the ice shelf and holding it in its webbed feet whilst brooding it through the long Antarctic night.

ABOVE Many water-birds build nests which actually float, like this handsome Horned Grebe which is found widely both in North America and Europe. Grebes lay conspicuous white eggs and whenever they leave the nest they carefully cover the clutch with some of the nest material, partly to keep them warm, but also to conceal them from any passing crow.

RIGHT A Green Woodpecker about to regurgitate partly digested food to the chick at the nesthole.

LEFT The Eider Duck is found in North America and Northern Europe and Asia. The duck lines her nest with down plucked from her own breast, hence the origin of the stuffing of some eiderdowns.

The males of some kinds of birds build nests to which they try to attract the female. This is part of the courtship behaviour, an essential step towards pairing. Here an Australian Greater Bower Bird displays at the entrance to the bower he has built in an effort to entice a female, who is watching from a bough above the archway, to come down and enter the tunnel.

RIGHT This tiny Ruby-throated Humming-bird is the commonest and most widely-distributed hummer in the United States of America. It is only just over three inches in length, including the long bill and tail. The nest is woven from dead leaves or similar material, often held together by gossamer, and is so small that the cup is less than an inch in diameter – just big enough to contain the two white eggs the size of small peas.

The numerous vireos of North America are closely related to the New World warblers. They are mostly summer migrants and this Red-eyed Vireo, which builds a beautiful little nest suspended from the branch of a tree or bush, is one of the commonest and best known.

Many nests are beautifully constructed, none more so than the domed nest of the Long-tailed Tit, built of thousands of bits of lichen and similar material and often lined with hundreds of feathers.

ABOVE Since the once abundant Passenger Pigeon became extinct at the very end of the 19th century, North America has not been rich in either pigeons or doves. One of the commonest is this Mourning Dove, which is a summer migrant in the northern United States and Canada, wintering in central and southern North America. It builds a rather fragile nest in trees.

Herons are widely distributed in most parts of both the Old and New Worlds. The large Blue Heron builds a bulky nest of sticks, usually in trees, or tall, thick bushes. Hungry chicks seize the bill of the adult, tugging away until the old bird brings up a helping of partly digested food in a kind of ringing-the-gong-for-dinner act.

Ospreys usually build their nests at the top of a tall tree not far from water. The nest may be over three feet in diameter and two feet in depth, composed almost entirely of dead sticks, some of which may be as much as three feet long and over an inch in thickness.

Gannets are cliff breeders, and prefer to nest on narrow ledges where they cram into every available foot of space.

Osprey landing on its nest

Prairie Falcon

Collared Sparrowhawk

INTRODUCED BIRDS
RICHARD FITTER

The House Sparrow may have originated in tropical Africa but it has spread northwards over Europe and has long been associated with man's settlements. Often a pest, it has been introduced into many parts of the world and is common and widespread in North America.

In almost every part of the world there are birds, sometimes among the commonest, which have been introduced, often far from their native homes, by man. It was man who brought the House Sparrow to North and South America, the Skylark and Song Thrush to Australia and New Zealand, the Pheasant and Canada Goose to Great Britain, and the Common Mynah to Hawaii, to name only a few. It was man who carried the now often remote ancestors of these birds from their native homes to a new country.

Two of the most widespread of these species are the European House Sparrow and Starling, both of which now inhabit most of the civilized parts of the globe. The Starling, a native of Europe and Asia, may be found today in North America, Jamaica, South Africa, Australia and Fiji. In the United States, though it is still most abundant in the north-eastern States, it has made its way north to the Gulf of St Lawrence, south to the Gulf of Mexico, and west to the Rocky Mountains.

The story of the House Sparrow's spread has been admirably told by J. D. Summers-Smith in his recent monograph on this bird. It is believed that its ancestors lived in tropical Africa and spread down the Nile valley to the eastern Mediterranean region, where they first came into contact with civilized man and became his commensal. It was early man's discovery of agriculture that enabled the House Sparrow to learn to live in close association with human settlements, and to exist largely on the grain grown by men, both in the fields and as waste droppings around their houses. After that, the sparrow followed grain-growing man wherever he went, and probably arrived in Britain with our neolithic ancestors long before Roman times. Even by 1800, however, the House Sparrow had not occupied the whole of the British Isles; it was not till later in the 19th century that it appeared in many isolated districts in the Scottish Highlands and islands. On North Uist, for instance, the House Sparrow was not known until 1913.

Saw-whet Owl pounces on a mouse

But the spread of the House Sparrow in Europe, Asia and North Africa, though closely linked with human activity, has been a natural one, very similar to the much more recent spread north-westwards across Europe from the Balkans to Britain of the Collared Dove, another bird that is semi-parasitic on man's food grains. In most districts the Collared Dove is first seen in or near a chicken run, where it finds the corn scattered for the fowls an easy way of obtaining the food it needs.

In North and South America, Australia and South Africa, on the other hand, the presence of the House Sparrow is entirely due to deliberate human introduction. The process began when eight pairs were released in Brooklyn Park, New York City, in 1850. Though these actually died out, fifty more birds were brought over in the following year and these survived to become, together with many other sparrows released in various parts of the United States, the forebears of the millions of sparrows that now inhabit not only the whole of the continental United States itself, but much of Mexico, many West Indian islands and southern Canada. Cuba seems to have been populated by birds brought from Spain by monks in 1850. The first House Sparrows were brought to South America in 1872, to Buenos Aires, and today the whole of the southern half of that continent is populated by their descendants, again augmented by other later introductions.

House Sparrows were first brought to Australia in 1861, and to New Zealand five years later. Today most of New Zealand and Tasmania and the inhabited coastal areas of south-eastern Australia are all sparrow territory. When you add some small colonies in South Africa, established since about 1890, and various islands in the Indian and Pacific Oceans, including Hawaii, Mauritius and New Caledonia, it will be seen that the House Sparrow is now extremely widespread, largely as a result of human interference. One of the comparatively few recorded unsuccessful introductions of House Sparrows was when twenty-six birds from London were released in St Helena in 1880. A hundred years ago the House Sparrow had by its own efforts occupied about six million square miles of the earth's surface; today, mainly as a result of human introductions, it has doubled that figure and can now be found over one-quarter of the land surface of the globe.

Most successful introductions of birds have been deliberate ones, for accidental escapes rarely occur in sufficient numbers to ensure a large enough breeding stock. The natural hazards to a pair or two of birds in strange territory are so great that they are unlikely to survive for more than a few years. Many deliberate introductions are also made with too few numbers to ensure success. It is a good rule of thumb for would-be introducers that the more animals or birds or plants you start with, the greater are your chances of success. However, perhaps a word should be added here on the extreme undesirability of private enterprise in introducing animals and plants in strange countries. Many of the world's greatest pests, such as the rabbit in England and Australia, and the Starling and House Sparrow in North America, were gratuitously introduced by man. Even in countries where the government does not control or prohibit the introduction of alien animals and plants, the private citizen should be chary of upsetting the existing balance of nature by fauna and flora of his own choice.

BELOW The European Tree Sparrow is a smaller, beautiful sparrow without any of the bad habits which have made the House Sparrow such a pest to man. Attempts were made to introduce this charming little bird into the United States of America. Though these were successful, the species has failed to spread and is only found very locally in Missouri and Illinois.

RIGHT Like the Goldfinch and the Green-finch, the Chaffinch has been established in Australia and New Zealand. The female, here seen feeding young, is soberly dressed, but the cock in breeding plumage is gaily coloured. Both sexes have the conspicuous white wing bars.

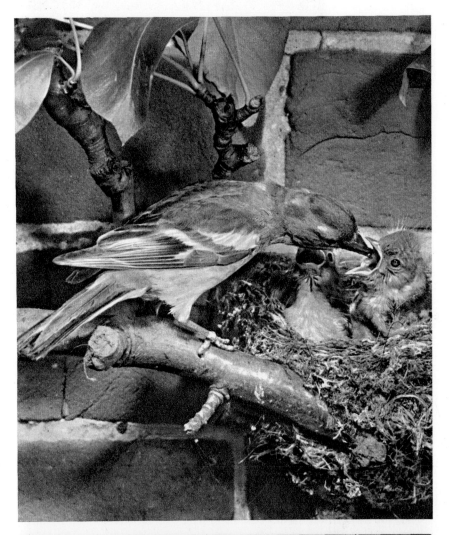

LEFT The Goldfinch was introduced from Britain into Australia and New Zealand. This charming bird with its crimson, white and black on head and bright gold in the wings, a lover of thistle seeds, was also introduced into the United States of America in 1878, and can be found on Long Island.

RIGHT The Song Thrush, which takes toll of so many snails in European gardens, is another bird introduced by settlers in New Zealand and Australia as a kind of living link with the homeland.

Three main motives have actuated the introducers of birds in various parts of the world in the past: provision or augmentation of game stocks, amenity or aesthetic reasons, and biological control. Of these, the most influential, in terms of numbers of birds successfully established in strange countries, have undoubtedly been the amenity or aesthetic reasons. The nostalgia of recent human immigrants for the sights and sounds of the mother country led, during the latter half of the last century, to many large-scale and often all too successful introductions of western European song-birds into North America, Australia, New Zealand, South Africa and the West Indies. Many English landowners in the 18th and 19th centuries imported large numbers of ornamental waterfowl to embellish their country estates, and descendants of many of these, notably the Canada Goose, still live wild in the English countryside. In western Europe, since at least the 17th century, and more recently in North America, chronic overshooting or overhunting of game stocks has led landowners and sportsmen to make substantial introductions of game birds, sometimes, as with the Partridge in Britain, to supplement the dwindling stocks of native birds, but more often, as with the Pheasant in both Europe and North America, to bring in completely new and alien species. The third reason, biological control of pests, has been much more rarely practised, but House Sparrows at least have several times been mistakenly introduced for this reason: to control plagues of caterpillars and other insects in New Zealand in 1866, and twice in South America with the same aim.

LEFT The Starling is one of the most adaptable and go-ahead birds in the world. It is equally at home on the bird-table, in the fields or on the lawn, where it does useful work in digging out many harmful insects. Introduced into the United States of America a long time ago, it is now common in the east. It has already spread westward to the Rockies and will probably continue to flourish.

FAR LEFT The Skylark has been successfully introduced into Australia and New Zealand from Europe. Immortalized in poetry by both Wordsworth and Shelley, the song of the Skylark is delivered from a considerable height and the cascade of beautiful musical notes is poured forth for minutes on end.

The very beautiful little Mandarin Duck was introduced into Britain from China as an ornamental waterfowl. It bred freely, however, and escaped birds have settled to breed in a wild state in several places. It is believed now to be more numerous in Britain than in its native country, an example of how by introducing a bird to a new area risk of extinction may be lessened.

In the British Isles attempts have been made to introduce more than a hundred different species of birds during the past century or so, but only four completely alien species have actually become naturalized in any numbers: the Pheasant, the Canada Goose, the Red-legged Partridge and the Little Owl. Many people believe that the Pheasant was introduced by the Romans, and this statement is repeatedly made in books and the sporting press on the strength of some bones found in Romano-British settlements, despite the fact that more than thirty years ago the late Dr. Percy Lowe proved them to belong to the domestic fowl. It may well be that the Romans did bring the Pheasant to Britain, but if they did we have no evidence that it escaped and established itself in the woods. The first documentary evidence of Pheasants in Britain occurs just before the Norman Conquest, and from that time onwards it is clear that Pheasants were spreading into the English woods, though not for several centuries more into those of Scotland or Wales. These so-called 'old English' Pheasants came from the Caucasus; more recent introductions have been mainly of the Ringnecked form from China.

The next alien bird to become established in Britain was the Red-legged or French Partridge, which seems to have been first brought into the country by King Charles II, at the end of the 17th century. It was not, however, until the end of the following century that a massive attempt at introduction by two Suffolk peers was successful. Today the Red-legged Partridge is commoner than the native bird in many parts of eastern England, and is spread more thinly over central and southern England.

Charles II also appears to have been responsible for the first Canada Geese in England, for the diarist John Evelyn saw some in his collection of exotic waterfowl in St James's Park, London. From the end of the 18th century many Canada Geese were allowed to fly free after they had been reared on country estates, but we do not know exactly when the bird became established as a feral breeder. Today it can be found in small colonies on lakes and ponds in the Dukeries of Nottinghamshire, the meres of Cheshire and Shropshire, the Breckland of East Anglia, the Thames valley around Reading, and several other parts of Britain. In 1953 there were some three thousand breeding pairs, according to a census conducted by N. G. Blurton Jones on behalf of the British Trust for Ornithology.

The fourth firmly established British alien breeding species is the western European Little Owl, which was turned down by landowners in various parts of southern England in the last quarter of the 19th century. This, too, is now firmly established as a breeding bird in most parts of England and Wales, and is just beginning to cross the border into Scotland. It is the smallest British bird of prey.

Five other introduced birds in the British Isles merit a brief mention. The Mandarin Duck, now breeding freely in Windsor Great Park, Berkshire, and a few other places, is said to be more numerous in Britain than in its native China. Both the Golden and Lady Amherst's Pheasants have been put down on various large estates from time to time; both have established themselves in a few places, the Golden notably in the Breckland of East Anglia and Lady Amherst's especially near Woburn Park, Bedfordshire, and in the New Forest. The Gadwall,

a European duck, has become established both in Surrey and East Anglia, as a result in the former case of escapes from the London parks, in the latter of deliberate introduction. The example of the Capercaillie in Scotland is somewhat different. This was a native bird which became extinct in the Highlands in the latter part of the 18th century, and was successfully reintroduced from Sweden within fifty years or so of dying out. Today this huge woodland grouse is once again a regular inhabitant of the pinewoods of Scotland, especially in the eastern half of the Highlands.

Of a different character again are the two domesticated birds that have re-established themselves as wild birds in many parts of the world. These are the Mute Swan and the Feral Pigeon. Mute Swans were probably quite wild in eastern England, as they still are in northern Europe, before they were more or less domesticated in the Middle Ages. During the past hundred years or so Mute Swans have broken bounds and spread over practically the whole of the British Isles as a wild breeding species again. The Feral Pigeon is descended from the wild Rock Dove which was also domesticated in the Middle Ages, and has escaped over the years to form feral colonies in the cities of Britain and many other countries.

France provides an interesting contrast to Britain, for the many introductions of birds there during the past century have all failed except for Reeve's Pheasant. The long established Common or Ring-necked Pheasant is the only other naturalized bird in France.

In North America, besides the successful and widespread Starling

Only a few species of geese regularly visit Great Britain and until the Canada Goose was introduced from America only one goose, the Grey Lag, nested. The Canada Goose was originally introduced as an ornamental fowl in the 18th and 19th centuries, but many birds are now breeding freely in a wild state.

The beautifully coloured pheasants are really natives of eastern Asia but this Ring-necked Pheasant is a popular bird with sportsmen, and has been brought into many countries, including North America, where it is found in southern Canada and in many of the northern and central states of the U.S.A.

and House Sparrow, small populations of Hungarian Partridges, Ring-necked Pheasants, Feral Pigeons and European Tree Sparrows and Goldfinches have become established. The Goldfinch was introduced at Hoboken, New Jersey in 1878, and within a year had spread to Central Park in New York City, and Englewood, New Jersey, where it established itself as a breeding species for thirty years or so. At about the time it disappeared from these two strongholds, it turned up on Long Island, which is at present its North American headquarters.

The homesick Britons who introduced song-birds into Australia and New Zealand during the last century had greater success than their North American counterparts. Today no fewer than thirteen species are naturalized in New Zealand and eight in Australia. The birds common to both countries are the Skylark, Song Thrush, Blackbird, Greenfinch and Goldfinch, as well as the ubiquitous House Sparrow and Starling. The two antipodean countries have also introduced species from other continents, among them the Indian Spotted Dove in Australia, the Common Indian Mynah in both (this species has been established in Hawaii as well) and the California Quail in New Zealand. The Asiatic Red-whiskered Bulbul is naturalized in south-eastern Australia, where it is common in town parks and is regarded as a pest by fruit growers. All those now at large are believed to be descended from a few that escaped from an aviary in Sydney. New Zealand also boasts of two introduced birds from Australia, the Black Swan and a magpie. Fiji suffers from introduced mynahs and bulbuls.

Birds cannot establish themselves in an alien land unless a whole range of factors, such as climate, food supply and sites for nesting and roosting, are more or less the same as in their native countries. And even when these factors, or most of them, appear to human eyes to be satisfactory, nevertheless some overlooked or extraneous factor often turns the balance the other way; for example, when an attempt was made some seventy or eighty years ago to introduce South American tinamous into Essex as an additional game bird, the local foxes killed the hen birds while they were sitting on their nests, and brought the experiments to an end.

It has been demonstrated that European birds can become successfully naturalized only in the parts of North America where the temperature and rainfall are similar to those in Europe where they normally breed.

In the special case of New Zealand, where so many European species have succeeded in establishing themselves, the native birds have been completely driven out of most of the cultivated parts of the country; this is because the European birds were already adapted to living in farmland, whereas the native birds mostly needed woodland or bush. It had taken European song birds such as the Blackbird and the Song Thrush several hundred years to adapt themselves to the cultivated farmland habitat; this period of adaptation was denied to the native New Zealand birds because the European ones were brought in too quickly.

Australia and New Zealand provide many interesting illustrations of the fact that when bird (or indeed any animal) populations build up to the point where the food supply is threatened, the surplus birds migrate overseas, even if their parents are sedentary. Thus many of the European song-birds naturalized in these two countries had already, before the end of the last century, appeared on the small islands of the seas to the southward, perhaps blown there by the wind. Today on Campbell Island, for example, there are Blackbirds, Song Thrushes, Starlings, Chaffinches, Redpolls and Hedge Sparrows all breeding. It was after a hurricane about thirty years ago that Starlings first appeared on Ono-i-Lau, a remote atoll in the Fiji group.

These movements do not represent true migration, but merely an urge to reach a less overcrowded habitat. The only instance of true migration developing in an introduced bird appears to be that of the Ring-necked Pheasant in Sweden, where it is no doubt due to the severe climate. Many migratory birds, on the other hand, have lost their migratory urge and become sedentary when transported to another country, for example the Canada Goose in Britain. Most of the European song-birds naturalized in North America, Australia and New Zealand belong to the group that are partial migrants in their home country. It is clear that any attempt to migrate southwards from Australia and New Zealand could only end in disaster, so that there is severe selection against migration and in favour of these birds remaining sedentary.

The largest grouse in the world, the Capercaillie, after becoming extinct in Britain in the 18th century, was successfully reintroduced and rapidly spread back in numbers to its old haunts. Three feet in length and with plenty of bulk, some birds are extremely aggressive and have been known to attack not only human beings and dogs but even automobiles.

The tiny Wren, after a successful foray, on the way back to a nestful of chicks with its tiny beak absolutely packed with an astonishing variety of insects.

Summer migrants from the south, the beautiful Cedar Waxwings are common nesting birds of North America. With handsome crests, yellow and brown plumage and waxy red tips to the wings, they enjoy various berries but also eat various insects and catch flies in the air.

BIRDS FEEDING

Many birds, like the warblers of both the Old and New World, live mainly on insects; others like the doves and the game birds are almost exclusively vegetarians. Birds-of-prey may eat rats, mice, voles and shrews and other birds as well as various small mammals. Other birds will specialize in snakes, lizards, frogs and toads, many enjoying a varied diet part animal, most vegetable.

No birds are more lovely than many of the New World hummingbirds. Most kinds, like this Sun Gem Hummingbird of tropical South America, are very small. They feed on the nectar of flowers or small insects in the flowers, always whilst in flight. The wings vibrate so rapidly, over fifty times per second, that they only appear as a hazy outline to an observer. Hummingbirds are unique in being able to fly backwards as well as forwards and they can also rise and fall vertically.

The medium-sized Hoopoe with its distinctive checkered plumage, down-curved bill and brownish black tipped crest gets its name from its loud cry 'Hoo-poo-poo'. Here the bird is carrying a small lizard into its nesting hole.

ABOVE Puffins nest in holes on cliffs on both sides of the North Atlantic, often in huge colonies. When fishing in the sea for food for its young a bird will generally collect six or more fish before returning to the nest, which poses the problem of how it manages to hold several live fish in its beak while swimming under water to catch another one.

ABOVE LEFT Some birds are expert fishermen, like this Belted Kingfisher of North America. Note from the picture how the wings are used in swimming under water, and how the eye is covered by the second eyelid or nictitating membrane.

LEFT The Herring Gull breeds commonly on both sides of the North Atlantic. It regularly frequents fish docks on the chance of getting an unearned meal. Here the bird has filched a mackerel from a Cornish fishing quay.

ABOVE A Garden Warbler feeding her week-old chicks in a bramble bush, a typical nest site.

ABOVE RIGHT This Common Buzzard at its tree nest is offering the leg of a frog to one of its three week-old chicks. Buzzards of many types are found in North America, common kinds being the Red-shouldered Hawk, Swainson's Hawk and the Red-tailed Hawk. Buzzards as a group are distinguished from other birds-of-prey by broad, blunt wings and rounded tails.

RIGHT Birds-of-prey seize their quarry in the sharp talons of their strong feet, instantly crushing the life out of them. Owls have very soft feathers which make no sound in flight, thus enabling them to pounce on their victims without warning as this Long-eared Owl is just about to do.

VANISHED AND VANISHING BIRDS

GUY MOUNTFORT

LEFT Dodos once inhabited three islands in the Indian Ocean. They were discovered early in the sixteenth century and being highly edible were mercilessly exploited. Being flightless they were easily clubbed to death and within two hundred years not one was left.

BELOW The flightless Great Auk, which only a few hundred years ago bred on cliffs on both sides of the north Atlantic, was ruthlessly exploited for food. At the opening of the 19th century it was almost extinct; the last bird was killed off Iceland in 1844.

Sailing the Indian Ocean five hundred miles off the coast of Madagascar in 1505, the Portuguese explorer Mascarenhas discovered the islands of Mauritius, Réunion and Rodriguez. Collectively these are now known as the Mascarene Islands. Dutch, British and French ships soon followed, for the islands provided plentiful food and water for seafarers. The chief attraction was an abundance of fat, flightless birds weighing up to 50 pounds each, which could be clubbed to death without effort and then salted down in barrels. The Portuguese sailors are thought to have called them *duodos* (simpletons), because they made little effort to escape, though this is only conjecture. We do know, however, that the Dutch called them *dod-aarse*. From one or other of these sources came the name Dodo. Today we lightheartedly use the phrase 'as dead as the Dodo' and this luckless bird has become a monument to man's shameful record of extermination of defenceless creatures.

From the day Mascarenhas first sighted the islands it required only 174 years for the flightless Dodos to be classified as extinct. Their evolution had taken place over hundreds of thousands of years; they had survived in a defenceless state because their island sanctuaries contained no dominant predators. Man hastened their extinction, as he has done countless times with other species, by introducing on the islands rats, pigs and monkeys, all of which eat birds' eggs. Today our only reminders of the Dodo are a few bones, egg shells and primitive drawings made at the time. Twenty-one other unique species of birds of the Mascarene Islands have also become extinct.

As often happens in the evolution of birds inhabiting island groups, the Dodos had developed into three distinct species. The one we call the Dodo was restricted to Mauritius. The White Dodo, or Solitaire, was found only on Réunion. The rather similar, though shorter-billed, Rodriguez Solitaire inhabited the island of that name and a few of them may have survived until the middle of the 18th century.

The history of the flightless Great Auk followed a similar pattern. Like the Dodo, it was of very ancient stock. Fossil remains found in Pleistocene deposits in southern Italy prove that Great Auks were living at least 60,000 years ago. They were evidently fairly numerous on rocky islands around the whole of the North Atlantic coasts, from Scandinavia and Spain to Greenland, Iceland and eastern North America. With the coming of European seamen armed with shotguns their days were numbered, for like the Dodo they offered easy food and bait and could be driven in flocks to slaughter. The first written description of the Great Auk, in 1684, referred to 'one they call the garefowl, which is bigger than a goose and hath eggs as big as those of an Ostrich'. The last pair was killed off the coast of Iceland in 1844; the last bird seen alive was in 1852, off the Newfoundland Banks.

Turning to more recent times, we have the more horrifying example of the American Passenger Pigeon. These beautiful birds were described a hundred years ago as so numerous as to 'darken the sky'. In 1871 a single flock was estimated at two and a quarter million birds; the breeding population of one area in Wisconsin was put at 136 million. Yet only thirty years later, after a slaughter probably unparalleled in human history, the wild Passenger Pigeon was extinct. The last surviving captive bird died in the Cincinnati zoo in 1914. Some impression of the process by which so numerous a species could be exterminated in so short a time can be gained from the records. A small town in Michigan shipped twelve million Passenger Pigeons to market in 1869. The markets became so glutted that tons of birds had to be fed to pigs, the hunters eventually not bothering to pick up their victims. Farmers meanwhile were dynamiting the breeding colonies in order to keep the birds off their crops. Nobody appeared to realize the probable outcome until it was too late. Another species had gone for ever.

North America has the unenviable reputation of having exterminated more species of birds in the past two hundred years than any other continent. Some, such as the Passenger Pigeon, Heath Hen and Carolina Parakeet, were destroyed before bird protection became a public issue. Others are still disappearing in spite of vigorous efforts to protect them. The California Condor had a population estimated at six hundred in 1950; today, thanks to poison and the shot-gun, there are certainly fewer than one hundred left. The Whooping Crane, which has probably had greater efforts expended on its protection in recent years than any bird in history, has continued to fall victim of the shot-gun; its total population is now numbered at over fifty. They are now breeding in zoos too.

But shooting is by no means the only cause by which a species

ABOVE The last surviving Passenger Pigeon died in the Cincinnati Zoo in 1914.

ABOVE LEFT Formerly a common bird in North America, the Whooping Crane population fell to just over twenty birds, and although desperate efforts are being made by the Audubon Society to protect this fine species, a census in 1968 yielded only forty-three wild Whooping Cranes.

Following pages

Pucheran's Emerald Hummingbird

Whooper Swans and cygnets

Red flamingo. *The Birds of America* by James John Audubon. (London, 1827–1838)

ABOVE The fashionable 'osprey' plumes come not from Ospreys but from egrets. These fine plumes can only be obtained from adult birds in the breeding season. The adult birds are slaughtered, and the choice plumes pulled out, the young being left to die. Although traffic in plumes is declining, this barbarous slaughter still continues in some countries.

ABOVE RIGHT The extremely beautiful Great White Heron is another species which has been persecuted, being exploited for the trade in millinery.

Blue Magpie from China. *The Birds of Asia* by John Gould. (London, 1850–1883)

becomes extinct. Often the reason lies in the destruction of the habitat in which it lives, many birds having developed preferences which are too narrowly specialized for survival among men. The strikingly beautiful Ivory-billed Woodpecker, which was regarded as extinct in North America in 1950, is an example. This bird depended on heavily forested and flooded land, in which the dying trees harbouring its favourite food were plentiful. Such habitats are rapidly disappearing under the land reclamation projects of Florida and Louisiana, where the last survivors have been seen. A few Ivory-billed Woodpeckers probably exist in the Oriente Province of Cuba and a few pairs are still surviving in Louisiana. Once these have gone another species will be struck off the world's list.

Birds inhabiting islands throughout the world have suffered particularly heavily. Only a few of the many species which have become extinct were flightless and therefore obviously vulnerable: for example, certain rails and emus and the earlier moas of New Zealand. From the Pacific islands at least thirty-three species or distinctive subspecies have disappeared during the last two hundred years and seventy more are approaching extinction. The Hawaiian islands alone have lost twenty-six and the islands of the Indian Ocean twenty-eight. Twelve have gone from the West Indies and judging by the almost complete lack of effective legislation in, for example, Jamaica, many more will soon follow. The few islands of the South Atlantic have lost only one species, the Tristan Coot, but at least two other species are now classified as probably extinct.

There were of course many additional lost island species which are known to science only from bones. These probably died out before the coming of man. The tragic fact remains, however, that sixty-eight per cent of all known losses to wildlife have occurred during the last century and that thirty-eight per cent were lost within the last fifty years. Nothing we can do will ever bring back a lost species, but we could undoubtedly still save a hundred or more birds which are now classified as nearing extinction. We could, that is, if we were prepared to make the effort in time and if money could be found to meet the cost.

Some species of birds have already been reduced to such small numbers that the only realistic solution would be to breed from them under ideal conditions in captivity. An admirable example of how this can be done is provided by the case of the Nene Goose of Hawaii.

Only thirty were left by 1950. Then J. D. Smith at Pohakuloa (Hawaii) and Peter Scott at the Wildfowl Trust grounds in Gloucestershire succeeded in rearing Nenes in captivity. Already thirty British-bred birds and five from Pohakuloa have been released in a sanctuary on the island of Maui where, in the absence of their chief enemy, the mongoose, they are thriving. It is planned to build up the flock to at least one hundred in the next two or three years.

Other disappearing species could be preserved by turning their breeding ground into guarded refuges from which such deadly predators as introduced mongooses, rats, cats and pigs have been excluded. The damage done by animals artificially introduced into a hitherto balanced ecological community is typified by what happened on Ascension Island. In 1815 the Royal Navy introduced a few domestic cats in order to control the rats which had come ashore from the ships. Within eight years the cats were running wild and had multiplied enormously. An official report written at that time mentioned that all

ABOVE One of the largest woodpeckers in the world, the Ivory-billed was once common in the south-eastern States of the U.S.A. and in Cuba.

ABOVE LEFT In many countries in Europe and North Africa hundreds of thousands of birds are still slaughtered annually to satisfy gourmets or to meet the huge traffic in cage birds. The beautiful Turtle Dove mentioned in the Song of Solomon is a summer migrant to northern Europe where most countries give it protection. Yet during the fortnight in spring when great numbers pass through the islands of Malta and Gozo as many as twenty thousand birds may be shot or trapped.

ABOVE The quizzical expression of this Eagle Owl may be coincidental, but he might well wonder what the future prospects of his kind may be if man continues to spread poisons indiscriminately over land and water.

ABOVE RIGHT The Tawny Owl is another rodent-hunter which is killed by poisons. Man is stupidly murdering some of his best allies.

the rats and most of the domestic geese, hens and turkeys had been killed by feral cats. During the following thirty years these animals, secure in their inaccessible lairs in the island's great larva beds, wiped out hundreds of thousands if not millions of nesting frigate birds, boobies and bo'sunbirds. Today only the Sooty or 'Wideawake' Terns breed in any numbers on Ascension Island, all the other sea-birds having been forced to withdraw to safety on the off-shore stacks or inaccessible cliffs. Similarly, the introduction of the mongoose to kill rats on the Pacific and Caribbean islands had appalling results in terms of losses to the indigenous wildlife and they still dominate many of the islands.

Large birds such as eagles and cranes, which wander far and demand extensive breeding territories, can be saved from extinction only by strictly enforced international legislation against shooting and egg collecting. It is no use giving a bird protection in one country if it is going to be shot the moment it flies over the frontier. Many countries have bird protection laws, but in very few of them are they effectively enforced. Some 'sportsmen' and gamekeepers still shoot every bird-of-prey they see, in the belief that they all kill game-birds, which is, of course, untrue. The European Short-toed Eagle, for example, feeds almost exclusively on snakes and lizards. It is now everywhere disappearing. As it lays only one egg each year it has little prospect of surviving the remorseless shooting. The white-shouldered Spanish Imperial Eagle, probably the most handsome of all eagles, feeds chiefly on rabbits; shooting and the destruction of its all-too conspicuous nests by peasants have brought its total surviving numbers down to fifty pairs. The Monkey-eating Eagles of the Philippines are also close to extinction, not from shooting so much as from collecting for foreign zoos, which offer high prices for the few survivors.

Very occasionally a species thought to be extinct is rediscovered. Two welcome examples were the Cahow, or Bermuda Petrel, and more

The Sparrowhawk, until recently so common in Britain that it was 'outlawed', is now extinct in many areas and a great rarity in many others. So grave was the status of this once common hawk that in 1963 special government orders were made giving it legal protection throughout Great Britain.

LEFT The spectacular Bateleur Eagle of Africa is still quite common. It is largely a scavenger. Hitherto the gravest threat to its future seemed to lie in development of the wild country which it frequents but unless some pesticides are controlled even species living in remote areas may be affected before long.

recently the Noisy Scrub Bird of Australia, of which a little colony has been found near Perth. On such occasions it is important that immediate action is taken to protect the breeding areas, particularly from collectors.

The mass killing of small song-birds as delicacies for gourmets, as practised particularly in Italy, Cyprus and the Lebanon, is a serious problem. The killing is completely unselective. Tens of thousands of migrant birds die a lingering death in bird-lime and nets in these and other Mediterranean countries. Thousands more are trapped for the cage-bird trade while migrating through Malta, Belgium and North and West Africa; seventy per cent of these die within a few days.

The threat to our vanishing birds is by no means limited to deliberate persecution. Often it is caused inadvertently by human enterprises. When ships discharge oil into the sea when cleaning bunkers or by accident, multitudes of sea-birds are condemned to die, unable to fly and with plumage smothered in sticky oil. Often the beaches of Europe and America are strewn with dead and dying sea-ducks, auks and guillemots from this cause. Legislation stimulated by the International Council for Bird Preservation to minimize these losses has been accepted by most maritime nations, but not yet by other countries, which operate some of the largest tanker fleets in the world.

In Bulgaria there has been a catastrophic decline in the populations of all birds-of-prey. As in most countries within the Soviet sphere, the shooting of wild birds is well controlled there. However, in order to reduce the losses of sheep and cattle killed by wolves, the Bulgarians

The Peregrine, one of the largest and most dashing of the falcons, has suddenly declined catastrophically in numbers both in Europe and America. In Great Britain alone the population has more than halved in a period of three years. Many of the remaining pairs fail to breed. Analysis of an addled egg showed the presence of persistent poisons.

LEFT The Black Kite, a useful Old World scavenger, is still numerous, yet its future is uncertain. Recently large numbers were killed in Israel by feeding on mice which had been poisoned by Thallium.

introduced the widespread use of poisoned bait. This lethal meat was inevitably eaten by eagles and vultures. Out of nine species of eagles and four vultures which used to inhabit that country, only four of the former and one of the latter remain and all of these are now scarce.

Since 1960 a sudden decline in the numbers of birds-of-prey has also been noted in Britain, the United States, Germany, Austria, Sweden, Finland and Israel. America's national emblem, the proud Bald Eagle, is among those affected. In Britain it is the Peregrine and Kestrel which have chiefly suffered. Evidence is accumulating that poisonous insecticides, herbicides, growth inhibitors, fungicides and defoliants may have been responsible. Eagles and Ospreys are known to have been feeding on fish poisoned by chlorinated hydrocarbon and organophosphorus sprays used on seashore and lakeside vegetation. Laboratory experiments show that one part per million of these chemicals in the food of a bird such as the Quail is sufficient to make it lay infertile eggs.

In a lakeside area in Connecticut only one pair of Ospreys out of thirty raised young in 1961, all the remainder having laid infertile eggs. Most of the Bald Eagles are also now failing to hatch their eggs. In Scotland the egg of a Peregrine was found to contain significant quantities of Dieldrin, DDT and Heptachlor. These poisons were undoubtedly transferred to the embryo by the parent bird having eaten Wood Pigeons (its chief prey) which had obtained sub-lethal doses from chemically treated grain. It is suspected that the steep decline of Kestrels in Britain is due to the eating of poisoned grasshoppers and beetles on sprayed farmlands. Nineteen dead hawks and owls were examined in 1962 and found to contain insecticide residues. In Israel the great reduction in numbers of Spotted Eagles, Black Kites and Long-legged Buzzards has been caused by their feeding on mice poisoned by Thallium. Elsewhere in the Middle East many White Storks have died after eating poisoned locusts. Unsuccessful attempts to control Dutch Elm disease by chemical spraying in the United States resulted in the almost complete extermination of wild birds over a large area.

Crop spraying and the chemical control of insect pests have greatly increased the productivity of farming throughout the world, to the unquestionable benefit of mankind. In an age in which two-thirds of the world is hungry, it would be idle to suggest that humanity should not reap the rewards of improved agricultural technology. What is needed is a wiser use of these dangerous products, for most of the damage is caused by over-dosing, or lack of precautions to safeguard wildlife.

The other great cause of losses among birds is the encroachment of man on their living space. Species such as the bustards, all of which are dying out in Europe, Africa and Asia, need wide-open plains for nesting. In Hungary, long the chief stronghold of the Great Bustard, mechanized collective farming has reduced the wilderness of the Great Plain to a fraction of its former size. The same thing has happened to the Dobruja steppe in Bulgaria, where this species used to be plentiful. The Great Indian Bustard and the Houbara Bustard of Arabia, on the other hand, are being wiped out by persistent shooting, rather than by the loss of breeding space.

Increasingly scarce birds such as the Dalmatian Pelican and Great Egret once bred in great numbers in the vast reed-beds of the Rumanian delta of the Danube. Peasant fishermen have for generations waged war on the pelicans, while the plume-hunters all but exterminated the egrets at the turn of the last century. Today both these species and many others are endangered once more by the annual cutting of the reed-beds for industrial production of cellulose.

One could easily draw up a list of birds nearing extinction which could be saved merely by stopping their deliberate destruction by man. This applies particularly to the rare ducks and geese which are shot for sport or food; or to the rare parrots, parakeets and finches which are caught for sale as cage-birds. Other rarities with known and restricted breeding areas could be saved by protecting these sites. The Steller's Albatross, the conspicuously crested New Caledonian Kagu, the Manchurian Crane and the unique New Zealand Takahe are examples. We could save the Hawaiian, Laysan Island and Marianas Island Ducks and the flightless Lord Howe Island Wood Rail by getting rid of the rats and cats which prey on their eggs and young. The few exquisite honeycreepers which survive on certain Pacific islands could be saved by excluding the introduced rabbits which have almost destroyed the vegetation on which these birds depend.

These are a few examples taken at random. We can clearly see what is happening to our vanishing birds. We know how we could minimize the consequences. We have a moral responsibility to act. But Albert Schweitzer has pointed out that 'the great fault of all ethics hitherto has been that they believed themselves to have to deal only with the relationship of man to man'. Do wild creatures have the right of existence only at the whim of man?

The Spanish Imperial Eagle with its distinctive white shoulders is another magnificent bird which is being ruthlessly persecuted. It is believed that the population has now been reduced to only fifty pairs. Unless the present disastrous trend is reversed, it could be extinct before the end of this century.

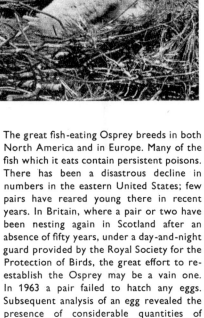

The great fish-eating Osprey breeds in both North America and in Europe. Many of the fish which it eats contain persistent poisons. There has been a disastrous decline in numbers in the eastern United States; few pairs have reared young there in recent years. In Britain, where a pair or two have been nesting again in Scotland after an absence of fifty years, under a day-and-night guard provided by the Royal Society for the Protection of Birds, the great effort to re-establish the Osprey may be a vain one. In 1963 a pair failed to hatch any eggs. Subsequent analysis of an egg revealed the presence of considerable quantities of Aldrin, Dieldrin and DDT.

Skilled conservationists in many lands have for years known what is needed to be done. That they have not acted is due to two reasons — lack of money and lack of interest by those who could provide it. Twentieth century man is more interested in reaching into outer space than in saving what is left to his own planet's natural heritage. The price of one lunar rocket, or a fraction of one per cent of what we spend on one year's gambling, would solve all the urgent problems of wildlife conservation.

Wildlife emergencies are nearly all man-made. Human population pressures and the inevitable demand for land reclamation, combined with increasing engineering skills and the needs of recreation, are factors easy to understand. Less easy to comprehend are the elements of wanton destruction of, and disregard for, wildlife. But in the past few years scientists, engineers, naturalists, land managers, businessmen and educationalists all over the world have been discussing more sensible ways of exploiting the earth's riches. The International Union for the Conservation of Nature and the International Council for Bird Preservation have played a leading part in this. From these deliberations has emerged the World Wildlife Fund. This is a kind of modern Noah's Ark, built by people of all nationalities, who give what they can to a central fund, out of concern that their children's children may continue to enjoy the pleasure birds and other wild creatures give them. The headquarters of the Fund are in Switzerland. Prince Bernhard of the Netherlands is the very active President. Great Britain, the United States, Switzerland, Germany and Holland have already launched

appeals. Enough money has been raised to enable some of the more urgent conservation projects to be started in regions as far apart as Malaya, Iceland, Tristan da Cunha, and the Galapagos Islands. Soon, it is hoped, every civilized country will be joining in a supreme effort to save what is left of the world's vanishing wildlife.

As it feeds entirely on snakes and lizards the Short-toed Eagle merits protection which it does not get. The European population is steadily declining.

RIGHT The Andean Condor, the world's largest flying bird, sometimes reaches a wing span of over eleven feet, and weighs around twenty-five pounds; it inhabits mountain tops, and is extremely rare.

YOUNG BIRDS

Ostriches lay about eight or ten eggs, each weighing over a pound. This newly-hatched chick looks bedraggled, and for a few days will be very unsteady on its legs, but will grow rapidly and soon be able to walk and even run. This is important because, being flightless, Ostriches rely on their speed to escape from their enemies.

Young birds are often very different from their parents. Newly hatched Gannets are covered in white down which is soon replaced by black speckled feathering and it will be three years before the chick acquires the mostly white adult plumage, pictured here with a well grown chick.

LEFT A cygnet nestles against its mother

ABOVE The young of the big group known as wading-birds hatch out chicks which can see from birth and are well-covered with down. These chicks seldom remain in the nest for more than a few hours, feeding themselves and only relying upon their parents to brood them at night and in cold or wet weather or to protect them against predators. Many chicks are most attractively marked, like these young European Curlews.

LEFT Penguins are birds of the Southern Hemisphere, though they are known everywhere through collections in zoos, where they are always popular. Unable to fly, they waddle about using their flippers like arms, often looking strangely human. This Gentoo Penguin with her chick is one of the medium-sized penguins and lives in the Antarctic.

ABOVE The young of most small birds, like these Magnolia Warblers of the United States of America, remain in the nest for less than a fortnight, but they are still dependent on their parents to supply them with food for at least another week or ten days. Yellow is a dominant colour in most American warblers and the Magnolia is no exception, with its bright yellow underparts contrasting with black and white wings and tail.

The small Fairy Tern inhabits tropical islands in the Pacific and South Atlantic. Here seen with its chick, this is one of the most beautiful members of an attractive family.

Newly-hatched chicks of the largest group of all, the passerine or perching birds, are born naked, blind and helpless. This nestful of Blue Jays, although nearly a week old, still have not opened their eyes but open their beaks and scream for food when they hear a parent approaching. They can be made to react in this instinctive way simply by gently rustling foliage near the nest.

Young owls often vary a great deal in size because the eggs are usually laid at two day intervals and incubation often starts on the first one. So in a brood of five there may be more than a week's difference in the age of the youngest and oldest chick. In this Barn Owl family it is quite easy to grade them by age.

Following pages

Brown Thrasher with young

American Robin with young

Yellow Warbler with young

BIRD-WATCHING

BRUCE CAMPBELL

Both in Britain and in the United States of America organized counts of various species of birds by amateur ornithologists are throwing more light on complex population problems, the effects of severe winters and droughts, toxic chemicals used in agriculture and changes in environments due to modern developments.

Japanese silk painting. Musée des Arts Asiatiques, Paris.

Bird-watching is still the cheapest sport in the world, its essential tools being the built-in senses of sight and hearing, plus a notebook and pencil. Binocular field-glasses are nearly essential; but for some kinds of observation (for example, when looking for nests in thick woodland), they are actually a handicap; and the housewife at her kitchen sink, who probably has more opportunities to watch birds than anyone except a professional ornithologist, needs no visual aids: her subjects come to the window-sill a few feet away.

It is of course possible to spend a great deal on equipment to photograph birds or record their songs, and even more on experiments in orientation which may end up in the construction of a planetarium with an artificially rotating sky; and travel can be expensive since birds are found from the tropics almost to the poles, all over the seas and high up the mountains; they fly high too, but can seldom be observed at an altitude except on radar screens. Birds also penetrate to the heart of the city where the cooing of pigeons and the chirping of sparrows accompany the tapping of typewriters and the battles of the boardroom.

The presence of birds wherever men live and work gives them one great advantage over other forms of life as a subject for amateur study; they also have the advantage over plants of moving, over insects and other small animals of being big enough to see, over fish of being terrestrial like man, and over mammals of living, again like man, mainly by day. All these combine to make bird watching or ornithology easily the most popular branch of natural history.

The majority of the 8,600 different kinds of birds in the world inhabit tropical Africa and South America, but bird-watchers are concentrated in the English-speaking lands and in Europe, and observers from these countries have told us most of what we know about the bird life of other regions. Bird-watching, like most civilized hobbies, is a product of the Renaissance and began in England in the 16th century, because there for the first time since the Roman Empire were to be found both peace and leisure in a fertile intellectual soil. Some facts were known about birds: they were either good to eat or considered to be enemies of crops and game. Some information had descended from the speculations of the ancients, and something — but much of it inaccurate — was known about the familiar birds of the countryside: one legend made Cock Robin the husband of Jenny Wren. But no-one had any idea of how many kinds of bird there were even in a small country like England, where they nested or what they did with themselves at other times of the year. William Turner, Dean of Wells, has been called the father of British ornithology; from his time onwards the work of studying birds systematically went on until by the end of the 18th century, when the plant and animal worlds had been classified on the system we still use by the Swedish botanist Carl von Linné (Linnaeus), a quiet Hampshire parish produced in the Reverend Gilbert White the prototype of the modern bird-watcher.

But though White's letters, collected as the classic Natural History of Selborne, are not unlike those exchanged by his 'descendants' today, White was not a bird protector; if a Stone Curlew flew up during a Partridge shoot, down it went. It did not occur to him that such birds might ever become rare or extinct. Nearly a century was to pass after his death in 1793 before societies in Britain, Europe and North America were strong enough to tackle the problem of saving birds from man's greed and exploitation. Even when the first laws were passed, they were largely honoured in the breach and there was a wide gulf between the 'bird-lovers' and the ornithologists who were still mainly concerned with 'obtaining' specimens. Although the modern bird-watcher owes his tradition of first-hand observation to Gilbert White, his preoccupation with conservation and reluctance to shoot birds are quite recent developments.

Shooting birds for scientific collections is necessary today in some parts of the world, where new species may even now be identified, but the whole emphasis of study is on the living bird, on its habits, behaviour and ecology or relationship to the total environment: geology, soils, weather and climate, plants, other animals and other kinds of birds; and since birds are predominantly dependent on the vegetation which gives them cover, nest sites and often food, the modern ornithologist has to be something of a botanist. But his first task is to learn to recognize birds in the field accurately and many people do not aspire beyond this: it is enough for them to identify birds and enjoy them. They make up the mass of bird-watchers and it is due to them that the research worker now finds a relatively favourable climate of opinion in most countries of the world.

The early stages of bird identification can be made much easier if the novice has an experienced guide who will point out the commoner species, the marks that distinguish them, their songs and calls, and the places where they are to be found. He can then read up about them at home in good field guides, with which Europe and North America are well supplied; other regions are gradually acquiring theirs. But it is a mistake to bring a book into the field and to try to look up an unfamiliar bird on the spot; it is only too easy to let bright pictures

Photographing birds often demands elaborate hides or blinds like this one erected at a Blue Jay's nest.

'Kitchen sink' bird-watching can be made even more successful with the provision of a window-sill tray or a bird-table well stocked with assorted foods. But remember that if you feed birds you will attract unusual numbers to your garden, so if you have to go away always arrange with a friend or neighbour that regular rations are provided. These Evening Grosbeaks are enjoying a fine feast.

influence your judgment, which will plump for the rarer of two alternatives. Far better to take down clear notes at the time and then work out the identification afterwards.

Full notes include the date, time, weather with wind directions and force, locality and habitat (for example: 'edge of mixed oak woodland and fields'; 'sandy seashore at high tide'; 'bullrush' swamp surrounded by junipers'). The bird itself is best described by making a field sketch, however rough, and indicating on it the colours of different plumage areas. Length, shape and colour of legs and bill are important; eye colour is worth noting if you can see it, plus the colour of the skin rim round it, the 'orbital ring'. Other sketches can show the pattern of the wings and tail in flight; these often clinch the identification of ducks or waders. If the bird calls or is singing, some sort of description in words should be attempted; and any notes on its behaviour may be invaluable: the way it holds itself (its 'habit') and moves, how it feeds and on what, whether it is alone or with birds of the same or other kinds. The last may give a useful comparison of size, which is often difficult to judge for solitary birds. Finally there should be a note of the type of binoculars or telescope used, the distance of the bird from the observer and the visibility. Not all of this detail will be necessary every time, but if the record turns out to be one you would like to submit for publication in an ornithological journal, you will probably find that the editor needs as much evidence as you can give before he will accept it.

The success of an actual field expedition begins with proper clothes. Needless to say they should be hard-wearing and appropriate to the country: no bright colours and no very light or dark ones either, unless you are working in snow or at night. Since birds are believed to be particularly aware of the human head-and-shoulders silhouette, a bird-watcher ideally should carry some sort of masking head-dress, but I have not met anyone who does, except in countries infested with mosquitoes or other insects. Footwear should take account of the terrain: in Europe and North America, where hazards range from deep mud and sharp stones to snakes and poison ivy, waterproof rubber boots are almost a uniform, but they are clumsy and noisy, and lighter footwear is preferable.

When nest-finding, a light stick for probing the vegetation is essential; a mirror fitted on the end enables you to look into nests without disturbing the cover or tearing your clothes; and a stick has many other uses, from protection against fierce dogs to helping you over barbed wire fences.

The best visual aids for the bird-watcher in mixed country are probably a combination of binoculars and telescope, if not too cumbersome to carry all day. In the poor visibility that often obtains in the north temperate zone a specification of 7×50 for binoculars allows use all the year round and at dawn and dusk; it has great light-gathering power to make up for comparatively low magnification. You may prefer up to $10 \times$ or even $12 \times$ enlargement, but the quotient when you divide the first figure of the specification into the second should not be much less than 4; for example, 8×30, giving a quotient of 3.75, is just acceptable. In tropical countries — and as you grow older — light-gathering power is not so important.

If your field trip is on foot, you will need, as well as your visual aids, notebook and pencils (more than one to allow for accidents), a rucksack or bag to carry food, extra clothing and maps. In wild country a compass is essential, and other useful 'tools' are a pocket lens, small boxes for specimens (bird pellets, egg shells, feathers) and perhaps a bird-call. North American bird-watchers are experts at calling up birds by imitating Screech Owls or simply by making squeaking and sucking noises with mouth and hands. When Bill Drury of the Massachusetts Audubon Society did this for me in an apparently lifeless oakwood, we were soon surrounded by pairs of Chickadees, Yellowthroats, Scarlet Tanagers and Downy Woodpeckers and by a Kingbird, a Black and White Warbler, a Redwinged Blackbird and a Blue-grey Gnatcatcher. But such wiles generally do not work on European birds, though no-one has yet explained why.

Though nothing can beat the field trip on foot as an energetic yet relaxing experience, it is comforting for the less active and the elderly to realize that the motor car, in spite of its artificial appearance, makes an excellent hide or blind; birds will tolerate a vehicle bulging with binoculars, telescopes and their owners far closer to them than a single observer on foot. This has made the car trip standard practice in the more civilized areas of Europe and North America, while the coming of landrovers, beach buggies and other 'go anywhere' types of vehicle has extended the moving hide technique into every continent. I have identified about 225 different kinds of bird in Europe from a car, most of them while in motion. At rest the roof gives an added vantage point although the watcher is no longer concealed.

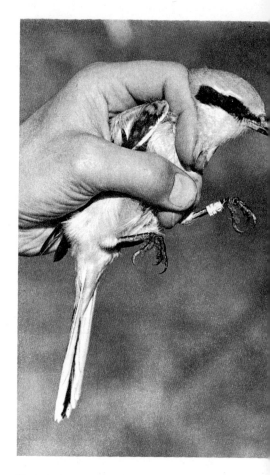

Bird-ringing – or banding as it is called in the United States – is an invaluable aid to ornithology. Small, metal, lightweight numbered rings are fitted to the legs of fledglings in the nest or adults caught alive in special traps. If a bird is subsequently picked up dead or caught alive in another trap, important details of its age and movements are obtained. Colour rings in various combinations make it possible to identify individual birds.

ABOVE The Robin of Europe is quite different from the American Robin. It is such an aggressive little bird that it hardly deserves to feature so often on Christmas cards as the messenger of goodwill. The traditional Cock Robin of the nursery-rhyme was killed by an arrow shot by the sparrow at the wedding between the Robin and . . .

ABOVE RIGHT . . . Jenny Wren. The Wren is in fact one of the smallest and most delightful of European birds, with a body no bigger than a man's thumb. But though the Wren is a great frequenter of gardens, it almost never comes to a bird-table, even in the hardest winter.

Some wonderful bird-watching can be done from ships. No ocean voyage is dull for an ornithologist and the Royal Naval Bird Watching Society has brought out useful guides to the birds likely to be seen along the most traversed sea routes at different seasons. There are limits to the deviation off course that a liner's captain is willing to make in pursuit of puzzling albatrosses, but small boats are almost as good as cars for approaching birds.

Bird spotting from trains has its own charm, and passes the time away magically; my first train ride in North America, from New York to near Boston, when almost every bird was a 'lifer' (life record) for me except the starlings and sparrows in the towns and the Mute Swans on the Connecticut bays, is the most memorable although the list of species seen was only about twenty. Aeroplanes are being used increasingly for special surveys of waterfowl and other big birds, and some years ago I took part in a three day flight over most of the offshore islands of Britain. Ostensibly we were looking for breeding colonies of Grey Seals, but we also passed over eight of the main British Gannet rookeries; the thousands of Fulmars criss-crossing the sea below us round lonely St Kilda was the most remarkable sight.

These remoter forms of bird watching eliminate what is perhaps its most skilled component: the recognition of songs and calls. While the bird-watcher can become familiar with the bigger birds of sea, shore, lake and open country without learning their notes, in wooded habitats he is at a great disadvantage if unable to identify the largely hidden life around by the audible clues it gives. The best way to learn is to go with a guide and then listen to the new songs and calls on one of the many gramophone discs of European and North American bird voices now available. But, excellent as modern recordings are, they cannot capture the high frequency songs with absolute accuracy; the European Robin, for example, always sounds slightly different in the field to the most faithful reproduction.

If you are alone when you hear a new song, you have the problem of describing it accurately in your notebook. The time-honoured method is to use an onomatopoeic word qualified by one or more adjectives; for example, 'a harsh repeated *churr*'; 'a mournful drawn-out *tsweep*'; 'a metallic twittering *chink chink*'. These lend themselves to facetious parodies but are often helpful. Unfortunately bird-watchers in different countries tend to pronounce notes differently: chew in English may become *chou* in French and *tschen* in German.

Sometimes quite poetic similes give a fair idea of a song: 'a jangling of little keys' for the Corn Bunting; or a phrase can be fitted to the sounds, like the 'please please please ta meetcha' of the American Chestnut-sided Warbler. Many American and some Australian birds take their names from their songs or calls. Whip-poor-will and Chuck-will's-widow are excellent for two nightjars but Phoebe is almost too ingenious, suggesting a classical origin rather than the call of an American flycatcher. Australia has its Kookaburra (a land-living king-fisher), New Zealand its Tui (a honeyeater) while Hawaii had its O-o, now feared extinct; Britain's Cuckoo is its best known example.

Now for a few final tips before you go into the field. Try to keep the sun behind you and if the wind will co-operate too, so much the better. Very windy, like very wet, days are likely to be unsuccessful for a bird-watching outing, though if you are operating mainly from a car, you can to some extent avoid the effects of the weather. If you are looking for nests, it is better to have the sun on the opposite side of the hedge or bush. When you put your head inside the canopy, the nests show up in silhouette against the light. Nest-finding is a skilled branch of bird watching and is useful for collecting information on breeding biology provided you take every care to cover up your traces and do not visit nests too often. Be particularly careful not to look too closely at broods of well grown young, otherwise you may cause them to leave the nest prematurely with disastrous results.

The kitchen-sink bird-watcher is not troubled by weather and hardly needs to be told nowadays to feed the birds so that they come readily to the window-sill or bird-table. Branded bird foods are now on sale in Britain and America but mixed scraps with seeds, nuts, fat, cheese and crumbled bread are a still useful diet. White bread and coconut should be withdrawn during the breeding season; the young of many small birds cannot digest them and tragedies may occur because the parents will take them to the nest — the white colour seems irresistible.

Having got together your simple equipment, a good bird book and, if possible, a well-informed friend or two, what should your first target be? In Britain there are about 75 resident and winter birds that are generally distributed and another 25 summer visitors arrive in spring; they make up a good century to start with, but at least 250 species are now recorded annually in the British Isles. Western Europe has about 450 birds of regular occurrence; eastern North America about 420,

LEFT Tree-stumps stuffed with nuts or fat will attract birds as readily as a bird-table. Woodpeckers, as well as finches, chickadees and nuthatches, have learnt to make full use of free issues, like this tiny Downy Woodpecker of North America. The pied plumage is relieved in males only by a red patch at the back of the head, and except for its smaller size and weaker bill, it is difficult to distinguish this species from the Hairy Woodpecker, another common American species which also comes to bird-tables.

RIGHT Fat on the top of a silver birch stump is just too tempting for this Blue Tit intent upon stuffing himself, whilst a Long-tailed Tit clinging to the other side of the stump seems to regard such gluttony with more than mild surprise . . .

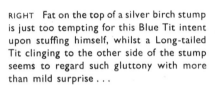

Peanut butter spread on a piece of toast will always attract birds. This Myrtle Warbler is trying an English breakfast of toast and marmalade in a Devonshire garden. The Myrtle Warbler is a common summer migrant in North America but this particular bird took the wrong turning in the autumn and crossed the Atlantic Ocean to winter in Britain – no mean journey for a bird weighing less than an ounce.

while the western states contribute another 200; Australia has about 700, but New Zealand has only 250, including a solid group of introduced European birds round the towns. The southern third of Africa has about 600 species.

But even while you are learning the fundamental skill of bird-watching, which is correct identification, you can begin on further simple studies such as a survey of the birds in your home area; some idea of their numbers and annual fluctuations is always useful because the status and distribution even of common kinds is continually changing, especially today under pressure from man's passion for 'development'. You can visit a bird observatory in Europe or a banding station in North America and learn how to measure birds and mark them safely with rings or bands; this also will help with identification. You can start on photography from a hide or blind, or you can take part in national and regional investigations such as those organized by the British Trust for Ornithology and the Massachussets Audubon Society. On holiday you can visit famous birding haunts and get to know new species; but as soon as you are reasonably proficient at recognizing them, look for somewhere more out of the way. Even in Europe there are areas which ornithologists seldom visit and where discoveries can still be made. This is something that bird-watchers (and naturalists in general) can claim against almost all other hobbies: with the minimum of equipment and expense it is still possible for the amateur enthusiast to add to the sum of human knowledge, and to help a little in raising the great curtain of ignorance about the world we live in.

Six species of pelicans still exist, four found in the Old and two in the New World. These Great White Pelicans live in Europe, Asia and Africa. Although big birds, they have long and beautiful wings and once airborne are strong fliers.

BIRDS IN FLIGHT

LEFT Greater Flamingos are impressive birds in flight, with their legs trailing almost as far out behind their bodies as their long necks and heads are in front. Indeed at a distance they can sometimes give a momentary impression that they are birds which are flying backwards. This flock have just risen from a shallow lagoon in the Camargue in the Rhone delta in the south of France – one of the most famous and important areas for birds in Europe.

Man has always been fascinated by the flight of birds, a fact which may have contributed to his own conquest of the air. Some birds, for example, many of the albatrosses and the swifts, spend the greater part of their lives on the wing, and are absolute masters of their element, but even very small birds undertake prodigious journeys when on migration. Many of the small warblers of the Old World, which may nest in the subarctic, spend the winter in the tropics and although weighing perhaps only one-third of an ounce have therefore to undertake two annual journeys of five or six thousand miles. The tiny Ruby-throated Hummingbird, which nests as far north as Canada, winters in Central America. Although weighing less than four grams, it undertakes a journey of several hundred miles over the Gulf of Mexico.

Gulls after launching into flight tuck their legs up into the feathers below the tail.

The Fulmar Petrel, a bird of northern waters which has increased greatly in the past fifty years, is another great traveller. Even when nesting it spends much of its time planing up and down on long stiff wings, riding the up-currents of air.

Whether they are large and heavy or small and light, birds when coming in to land adopt the same basic methods, using their wings as brakes, steering with their tails and lowering their legs ready for the landing. The Gannet, found breeding on both sides of the North Atlantic, as well as in Iceland, weighs many pounds and has to stall with its massive wings and brake with its tail as it prepares to land on a rocky ledge beside its nest, which contains a half-grown youngster.

Small birds in flight usually flap their wings too rapidly for the eye to perceive them properly. The camera, however, catches every detail of this Fox Sparrow, which nests in Canada and the northern United States.

The Barn Owl, a most useful bird found almost throughout the world, is here seen at the moment when it is plunging to seize its prey — wings held steady, tail fanned out to act as a brake and taloned feet wide open. The face suggests a moment of intense concentration — and it probably is, unless the owl wants to miss its dinner.

In flight tails are often as important as wings; this Raven is using its tail as a rudder to steer to the left.

BIRDS IN ZOOS

D. H. S. RISDON

The Great Northern Diver or Loon breeds in Arctic regions of America and Europe. Zoos afford an opportunity to see how diving birds hunt when under water; this diver is pursuing fish, swimming vigorously with his big, webbed feet.

Most of the zoos of the world have first rate collections of birds, well housed and displayed, and usually exceeding the other exhibits numerically if not in size and value. However, they tend to be eclipsed by mammals and reptiles because of the very size of the former and the 'horrific' associations of the latter. Beautiful though birds are they do not compete in the eyes of the general public with, shall we say, elephants, Giraffes or sea lions. It was for this reason that I decided to start the Tropical Bird Gardens at Rode in Somerset which is a zoo in which the birds are the main attraction.

The general interest in birds is very widespread; for example, bird-watching is one of the most popular hobbies today. At The Tropical Bird Gardens it was felt that if they had the stage to themselves they would really come into their own, and this is proving to be the case. People are noticing, perhaps for the first time, the sheer grace and beauty of birds, in their way as diverse in form and interesting in their habits as any other group of living things.

The idea was partly prompted by the great success of the 'Parrot Jungle' in Florida in the United States, which has now become internationally famous. Started in the mid-thirties by Francis S. Scherr, one of the unique features of the place is that most of the birds fly at

No zoo is really complete without its flamingos. The Greater Flamingo is a really large bird with a wing-spread of nearly six feet. When a bird stretches up like this one is doing, its head is about five feet high, which is quite something even if it is almost entirely neck and legs.

complete liberty. Many of them are trained to do tricks and the macaws and cockatoos are so tame that they will fly to the arms and shoulders of visitors who want to have their photographs taken with the birds. Besides parrots many other birds are exhibited including flamingos, Crowned Pigeons, ornamental waterfowl, peafowl, cranes and ornamental pheasants.

Another bird zoo which has become very well known in England is 'Birdland' at Bourton-on-the-Water in Gloucestershire, itself one of the show villages of the Cotswolds. Here visitors may see, in the surroundings of an English garden, a fine collection of exotic birds from all over the world. Penguins and also macaws flying at liberty feature prominently at this place.

Inevitably it is the quaint or the spectacular which attracts attention in the first place. Penguins will always be firm favourites: these amusing birds with their upright gait and curiously 'human' figures rank high in popularity in any zoo. But it is only on land that they remind us of ourselves; in the water they become birds again literally flying under water.

Penguins in zoos have to be taught that dead fish are food. At first they do not recognize this since they are of course used to catching live fish in the open sea. They have therefore to be fed at considerable risk to the hand that feeds them. Their razor edged bills with hooks at the end can inflict painful wounds.

Ostriches probably come next in popularity, with their striking height of over seven feet and their remarkable shape. They neither bury

ABOVE The Shoebill is a large stork found in tropical Africa and gets its name because it has one of the oddest bills in the bird world.

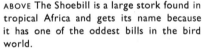

ABOVE RIGHT Pelicans are popular zoo birds. But if the rhyme, which suggests that they can hold in their beak enough food for a week, is scientifically inaccurate, some species have a beak capacity of several gallons; the 'bag' of loose skin under the beak acts as a fishing-net when scooped through the water.

their heads in the sand nor are they capable of digesting everything and anything, as is commonly believed: they will swallow the most unsuitable articles but probably as many Ostriches die from injury to their insides caused by 'foreign bodies' as from any other cause.

The late Herbert Whitley, who founded Paignton Zoo, once told me that in his opinion it was lack of suitable grit that caused Ostriches to swallow such things as padlocks, bunches of keys and bits of wire. Like many other birds they require grit to enable them to digest their food properly, but a bird the size of an Ostrich needs stones the size of marbles. Pebbles of this size are not always available in sufficient quantities in the average Ostrich paddock. He related how once he demonstrated this theory to a certain learned zoologist, who was somewhat sceptical, by offering one of the Paignton Zoo birds a bent, three inch nail. The bird merely ran the nail between its mandibles and dropped it. Needless to say it had all the grit it needed of the right size. When I was at Dudley Zoo I remember being present at a post-mortem on an Ostrich and seeing about two large handfuls of pebbles as big as marbles in its gizzard.

The story about the Ostrich burying its head in the sand probably arose because seen from a distance when feeding off the ground, the head was invisible to early travellers unfamiliar with the bird, who may have thought it had stuck it into the ground. Sometimes these birds will squat and stretch their necks flat along the ground, a habit which again at a distance may make the neck and head invisible.

Other large flightless birds which are usually kept in zoos

are Emus, rheas and cassowaries. All do well in captivity and live for many years, thriving on grain, bread, fruit, green vegetables and meat.

Birds in captivity are comparatively easy to house, at any rate in temperate climates, and the vast majority of them, even those from the tropics, after they have moulted become accustomed to cooler weather, provided that they are given adequate shelter from cold winds, snow and severe frost and provided of course that they are properly fed. Fresh air seems more important to them than the close atmosphere of a heated tropical house, and those which have access to outdoor enclosures all the year round invariably appear in better condition than those housed indoors.

Artificial heat is of course necessary for delicate species in severe weather conditions, but it has been found in practice that the best way of providing this is for the birds to have two compartments in their enclosures — one completely enclosed except for a small entrance hole and one entirely open to the elements. The enclosed part is warmed either by electricity or central heating so that the birds can remain inside when so inclined but can have access to the open air whenever they wish. This is the principle on which the birds are housed at the Tropical Bird Gardens.

Of course the reverse applies in warm countries where the problem of heating does not arise. There the problem is to provide shade. Birds, even those from the tropics, avoid hot sunshine when they can. They like it in the early morning and again in the evening but seek shade during the heat of the day. Birds from the Antarctic, particularly penguins, do not like hot weather, and in some zoos in America and in Germany they are kept in special air cooled enclosures.

The construction of bird enclosures, when compared with the elaborate and often expensive structures required for other zoo animals, is simple. For one thing birds do not require reinforced concrete or iron bars to keep them in. Wood and wire-netting are adequate materials although of course in the larger zoos the bird houses are often built of bricks and concrete for permanency.

Wood and wire-netting will keep birds within bounds but there is one exception, the parrot family. Parrots are born carpenters and the larger ones, particularly the macaws and cockatoos, with their strong beaks, will chew through exposed woodwork, rapidly reducing their enclosure to a heap of matchwood. They can also bite through wire-netting, so their aviaries and cages must be strongly built of heavy gauge chain link or welded wire mesh stretched on a framework of metal supports; if wood must be used it should be carefully covered with metal sheeting. A parrot uses its beak like a pair of pliers twisting and turning at wire netting until it has literally unravelled it and made a hole large enough to get through. This is not necessarily done in order to escape. At Rode there is a pair of Salmon-Crested Cockatoos — the largest species — which spend their time wandering about the grounds and trying to bite their way into aviaries housing other birds!

The larger birds which do not perch or climb are generally housed in open paddocks with a surrounding fence about six feet high. This is because they require ground space rather than height and can thus be given greater freedom. In fact such birds often share the paddocks of herbivorous mammals like antelope, deer or zebra. The paddocks in

A Turkey Cock. Inscribed by Mansur (Mughal, Jahangir period, 1612). Victoria and Albert Museum.

Hornbills come from tropical Africa and Asia and are represented in most zoos; they are distinguished by abnormal development of the upper mandible. The female nests in a hole and after she has settled to brood the male walls her in with mud, leaving only a tiny hole through which he feeds her on berries and other food, whilst she remains imprisoned during the month or more necessary to hatch the eggs.

The Stele of the King Serpent. Egyptian. First dynasty. Musée du Louvre.

this case must extend to several acres, as they do at Whipsnade and Chester Zoo. A typical birdhouse consists of a building in which cages are arranged round the walls; the centre is occupied by several larger aviaries, often planted with tropical foliage and decorated with ornamental rockwork and small pools. The temperature can then be controlled and visitors can view the inmates in comfort when the weather is bad outside.

Nowadays in order to give visitors an uninterrupted view of the exhibits modern zoos are doing all they can to eliminate intervening fences between the animals and the public. Unfortunately the ditches and moats which will keep mammals within bounds are no barriers to birds. Aviaries sufficiently spacious to enable visitors to enter and walk about among the inmates, with entrances and exits constructed with safety porches (to prevent the accidental escape of the birds), has been one answer to this problem. This method is proving highly successful but it is usually necessary to confine the visitors to a well defined footpath while inside the aviary for the sake of the birds. Anyone who has ever had practical experience of running a zoo will tell you that enclosures are quite as necessary to keep people out as to keep animals in.

Another method of exhibiting birds without visible barriers, and one which has found favour in America, is through the use of light and darkness. The theory is that birds will not fly into a dark space, so that if their cages are brightly lit and the exhibition hall itself is in darkness they will not attempt to escape.

ABOVE The Rhea hails from South America; like the Emu and cassowaries of Australia and the Ostriches of Africa, species to which it is closely-related, the Rhea is flightless but can run rapidly on its long and powerful legs.

ABOVE LEFT Cranes are not related at all to storks and flamingos. Strangely enough they are akin to the small Moorhens, coots, rails and gallinules. They are found in all continents except South America and New Zealand. These handsome Crowned Cranes, an African species, are about four feet high.

Whether birds are housed outdoors or indoors their enclosures have to be furnished according to their needs: perching birds need branches and twigs of the right thickness; owls and eagles like a stump to sit on; big birds like Ravens, hornbills or parrots may need perches several inches in diameter; tiny species like waxbills or hummingbirds prefer thin twigs, and many birds like pheasants which spend the day on the ground need perches for roosting at night; waders will require a pool and a damp marshy spot in which to probe for worms; forest dwellers like fairly thick cover. Ground-dwelling birds have tender feet which can be damaged if they are compelled to walk on hard surfaces like concrete or, worse still, concrete on which dry sand has been scattered. Natural soil is the best for these or a thick layer of granulated peat moss. The position of the perches in an enclosure is important. They should be so arranged that the birds obtain the maximum amount of exercise flying to and fro.

The feeding of birds in zoos is quite a problem, particularly among the smaller insectivorous species whose diet is not easily substituted. Those with similar diets to man are probably the easiest to feed although often the most expensive. Where it is impractical to provide an insect-eating bird with live food, a substitute diet is prepared which consists of all kinds of ingredients such as biscuit meal, soya bean flour, meat meal, egg yolk, shrimp meal, dried flies, ant 'eggs' and dried silkworm pupae. Some or all of these are mixed together in varying proportions, and vitamins and liquids are added until the whole mixture looks like a rather crumbly pudding. All the foregoing

Adjutant Storks or Marabous are natives of Asia and Africa. They often feed on carrion and so are frequently seen with vultures. They are large birds and can look quite active, like this preening bird.

materials are produced commercially for zoos and private aviculturists who keep insectivorous birds. Dried flies are not flies at all but a small species of water bug which is netted from ponds in vast quantities abroad and dried. Ant 'eggs' are in fact the cocoons of the ant and not its eggs. Dried silkworm pupae are a by-product of the silk industry, the chrysalids from which the surrounding cocoon and silk have been stripped. Mealworms are the larvae of a beetle which lives on flour and bran. They are bred commercially and sold by the pound especially for bird feeding. Maggots or gentles which are the larvae of bluebottles are similarly bred not only for bird feeding but for the fishing bait trade.

Quite a number of tropical birds such as hummingbirds, sunbirds and lories — a specialized group of parrots — live in a wild state on the nectar from flowers and fruit juices. For these an artificial nectar is concocted consisting of baby food, milk, honey and sugar diluted with water. Lories have specially adapted tongues with a brush-like arrangement at the tip which enables them to lap their liquid diet more like a mammal than a bird. Hummingbirds and sunbirds require live food as well, so for these cultures of *Drosophila* or fruit flies are grown.

No zoo would be complete without a collection of parrots. The ability of some of them to talk makes them firm favourites with visitors, although curiously enough many are reluctant to speak in front of people. Even so their tameness, their brilliant plumage, and their fondness for the human race are endearing. They seem to be genuinely affectionate towards human beings, although ornithologists will say

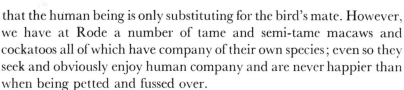

that the human being is only substituting for the bird's mate. However, we have at Rode a number of tame and semi-tame macaws and cockatoos all of which have company of their own species; even so they seek and obviously enjoy human company and are never happier than when being petted and fussed over.

Everyone knows the popular cockatoos and macaws and the larger parrots, but it is often not realized how many and varied are the different members of the parrot tribe. I am now using the term in its broadest sense. Parakeets, lovebirds, lories, lorikeets and conures are all basically parrots. Tiny species half the size of a Budgerigar, called Hanging Parrots because of their habit of sleeping hanging upside down from a perch rather like a bat, are other members of this diverse family.

Birds-of-prey usually form part of a zoo collection. Although they do very well in captivity, living for many years, they are not easy subjects to display well. They look their best in flight and it is only the major zoos which can afford really large flying aviaries of great height which can show them to advantage. In a confined space they appear clumsy and ill at ease although they survive well and sometimes breed. One of the feeding problems of birds-of-prey is providing them with sufficient roughage in their diet, which they cast up from their crops some hours after a meal in the form of pellets, the matted remains of the feather, fur and bones of their victims. Ordinary butcher's meat is eaten readily enough but part at least of their rations must consist of small mammals and birds like rats, mice, pigeons and chickens. Lack of roughage will cause digestive trouble and even death.

ABOVE The very rare Monkey-eating Eagle comes from the Philippine Islands; it is feared that the bird may become extinct unless immediate action is taken to conserve the dwindling population.

ABOVE LEFT Storks are closely-related to the flamingos. Outside zoos, these White Storks breed over much of Europe and Asia, many migrating south to Africa in the winter.

Sea eagles are magnificent creatures found in most parts of the world, from the tropics to the polar regions. This White-breasted Sea Eagle comes from Malaysia, Indonesia and the oceanic islands of the Pacific.

It is generally known that birds, having no teeth, swallow their food whole or in lumps. Those whose diet is of a tough or fibrous nature, like grain or leaves, need grit, which is swallowed and retained in the gizzard, where the grinding action breaks down indigestible matter before it is passed into the stomach for further digestion.

Not all birds, however, eat grit. Those which eat soft fruit, insects or meat would suffer internal damage if they did; the common practice of covering the floors of cages and aviaries with sand may have fatal results if pieces of fruit or meat are dropped on the floor, covered in sand and subsequently eaten.

Another thing the zoo keeper must provide is adequate bathing facilities. This is most important if the birds are to keep their plumage in good condition. Bathing is unfortunately only too often neglected, resulting in the dry and ruffled plumage of many birds kept indoors. Certain species dust bathe like pheasants, quail and other members of the chicken family, but the vast majority bathe in water, either by taking a tub like the birds at the bird bath in one's garden, or spreading their wings in a shower of rain, or ruffling their plumage in wet foliage.

Dust baths consisting of a mixture of earth, sand and ashes must be provided in dry spots in shelters or under bushes. Water baths should be shallow and wide enough for big birds to get right in and have a good splash. The water must be absolutely clean and fresh or the birds will not use it. In most climates those which take rain baths will get all they require if they have access to an outdoor aviary but those which live indoors in bird houses should be sprayed regularly.

141

This Sociable Vulture comes from Africa. With their bare necks, vultures are rather repulsive looking birds but they do well in captivity. As they are mainly carrion eaters, feeding them presents no problem.

BEAKS

ABOVE Herons, of which this Grey Heron is a common example, are found in most parts of the world; they are almost all fish-eaters wading slowly in shallow pools, hardly making a ripple, head craned forward, watching for a fish to stab to death with their dagger-like bills.

ABOVE RIGHT Birds-of-prey, like this famous Bald Eagle, have strongly hooked, powerful beaks. Although they strike, kill and carry their prey with their feet, birds-of-prey need this characteristic bill for tearing the flesh off their victims.

The beaks of birds are adapted to the uses required of them. They may be strong and thick, like those of finches and grosbeaks, for crushing large seeds or fruit kernels; they may be small and weak, as in warblers and other insectivorous species; and they may be pointed and strong for excavating nesting-holes in trees, like the woodpeckers, or sharp and long, as in the herons, for spearing fish. They may be straight or they may curve up or down, or they may be crossed at the tips. The diversity in this one feature alone is enormous.

Beaks of snipe are long, straight and slender, the most effective deep-probers of them all. The bill of this European Common Snipe is rather longer than that of two common American species, the Dowitcher and Wilson's Snipe.

The avocet is one of the few birds with an upswept bill, from which it gets its nickname of 'awl-bird'. This, the so-called European Avocet, is found from Britain to India and south into Africa. Apart from lead-blue legs, it is entirely black-and-white, whereas the otherwise similar North American Avocet has the head and neck of soft chestnut-brown in spring. Both species are amongst the most elegant and graceful in the world.

ABOVE The Hairy Woodpecker is a medium-sized member of this world-wide family, common in North America; it makes its own nest-hole, using its sharp, strong bill in the same way as a carpenter uses a chisel, excavating a chamber which may be twelve or fifteen inches deep.

ABOVE RIGHT These are African Spoonbills but closely related species occur in many parts of the world, including America, where one of the most beautiful – the aptly-named Roseate Spoonbill – nests in the extreme south-east of the U.S.A. All spoonbills have the long, strong spatulate bill with which they probe deeply in the mud for food, in a figure-of-eight fashion, as they march forward on their long legs.

The pelican is an enormous bird, having a wing-spread of six feet, an appetite to match its bulk and a bill large enough to serve its appetite.

Finches, being chiefly seed-eaters, need strong bills, like this Evening Grosbeak, a common species in the evergreen forests of Canada and the northern parts of the United States of America.

Pied Flycatchers feed only on small, soft flies and other insects, and so only require small, thin bills; this male is about to enter his nesting-hole with a good beakful of food for the chicks within.

BIRDS
IN THE HOME

D. H. S. RISDON

ABOVE Lovebirds are thick-set parrots found in tropical regions of the Old World. They make good cage-birds if properly cared for and pairs always seem to be especially devoted to each other, settling on a perch side-by-side and as close together as possible.

ABOVE RIGHT The Budgerigar has ousted the Canary as the commonest domesticated bird kept in the home and many attractive variants exist. In a wild state Budgerigars come from Australia, where they are very common and are called 'grass-parrots'. In spite of their diminutive size, they are closely related to true parrots.

Birds are widely kept as pets; the Budgerigar probably outnumbers the cat and dog in these days of small houses and flats where space is at a premium. But birds have certain advantages as pets over other animals. Contrary to popular belief they take kindly to captivity: they are comparatively easy and cheap to feed and house; they do not smell; they are colourful and gay and always give the impression of being cheerful.

The bird fancy is a thriving one. It is catered for in Britain by *Cage and Aviary Birds*, a weekly journal devoted to the hobby. The oldest Society is the Avicultural Society, founded in 1894, its object being to foster the care and breeding of all kinds of birds, especially the rarer foreign species. The Foreign Bird League has a similar aim but, as its name implies, specializes in birds from overseas. Membership is open to genuine bird keepers on payment of an annual subscription. Both publish a bi-monthly magazine containing articles of interest to their members. These societies have a world wide membership but apart from them practically every town in Britain has its local cage bird club which holds regular meetings at which talks are given and the problems of bird-keeping discussed. Most of them hold at least one show a year and competition is keen.

The great event of the year is the National Show of Cage and Aviary Birds held at Olympia at which the winners from all the club shows compete for final honours.

The National Council of Aviculture is a body composed of delegates from the various societies. It represents bird fanciers on a national basis and has done much useful work in dealing with government departments and local councils on matters of legislation, improvement in the transport of birds and giving advice to fanciers and societies on legal matters.

The hobby of bird keeping is equally popular in the U.S.A., Europe and the Commonwealth. The same species are favoured as in Britain, but bird-fanciers are fascinated by keeping birds which are not native to their own country, so inevitably foreign species are more popular than the 'home-grown' ones. Many birds are now protected by law in their native countries, which means that their export is prohibited except under special licence to *bona fide* zoological gardens. Conversely import restrictions may apply to prevent the introduction of diseases as in the case of parrots or species which might become pests. This applies particularly in countries like Australia and New Zealand where introduced species have gravely threatened native fauna with extinction.

Birds kept in the home may be broadly divided into two groups — those which live outdoors in the garden such as pigeons, bantams and aviary birds and those which live in the house like Canaries, Budgerigars, parrots and small passerine birds which do not require a great deal of space. These are collectively referred to as 'cage-birds'.

The Canary is said to have been domesticated for something like five hundred years. Wild Canaries, which are dull green in colour, still live on the Canary Islands, but their tame descendants are very different birds. They were undoubtedly originally kept for their sweet song, and today there is a breed known as the Roller, which is specially bred for this purpose. As with most domesticated livestock, variations and mutations have occurred down the centuries, so that the original shape and size of the bird has been greatly changed. The various breeds are named after the localities in which they were originally bred; for example, the Norwich, the Yorkshire, the Border, the Scots Fancy, the Belgian Fancy, the Lancashire Coppy and so on. Most people think of the canary as a yellow bird, but it exists in white, blue, fawn, cinnamon, green and orange. Those who wish to keep a Canary for its song should remember that only cocks sing, and consequently they are worth three or four times the value of hens. A cheap Canary is almost certainly a hen and will never sing.

The Budgerigar has become domesticated within the last half century. Before this thousands were exported from Australia, its native land, where it still occurs in a wild state. The original wild form is green, with a yellow head and wings marked with black, and a blue and yellow tail. Although the domesticated form has increased in size, its shape has so far only been slightly modified. It is, however, in the wide range of colour variations that the budgerigar breeder has excelled: this little parakeet now occurs in blue, mauve, cobalt, violet, yellow and white with many intermediate shades and patterns.

The Budgerigar's ability to talk has made it a very popular pet; a young bird, if taken indoors soon after leaving the nest, petted and cared for, often develops a vocabulary which surpasses that of the average parrot. In addition these birds make the most amusing and intelligent pets and show great attachment to their owners.

Although they make such good house birds, Budgerigars are perfectly

LEFT Aviculturists are always striving to produce new colour variations. This bird is known as a variant or mutant. It is a mutation from an ordinary Greenfinch, very pale, soft fawn in colour, quite unlike a normal bird . . .

BELOW LEFT . . . and this bird is a sister, an almost white bird, known in 'the fancy' as a 'lutino'. This breeder will now be able, by selective mating and inbreeding, to produce a variety of colours all quite unlike the original wild parents.

RIGHT Cockatoos, always handsome, usually large and often vividly coloured, come from south-east Asia, Australia and the South Sea Islands. They belong to the parrot family but are distinguished by their large crests which they use in various displays.

hardy, and will live outdoors all the year round in garden aviaries, where their bright plumage brings life and colour to many a garden. The late Duke of Bedford discovered in quite recent years that they could be trained to fly free like pigeons and return to their aviary for food and shelter.

Whereas these diminutive members of the parrot family are comparatively recent additions to the ranks of pet birds, the larger parrots have been kept in the home almost since the beginning of civilization. The ability to talk is undoubtedly the parrot's great attraction, which is, however, frequently offset by the bird's raucous voice. Parrots show great affection for their owners, and when given a reasonable amount of freedom develop remarkable personalities and show a high degree of intelligence.

The African Grey Parrot with a red tail makes the best talker, having a large vocabulary and clarity of diction. This bird can mimic the exact tone and accent of the human voice (often to the discomfiture of the person imitated). Many is the time that I have been fooled by a Grey Parrot calling me in the voice of a member of my family. These parrots show a peculiar shyness about talking in front of human beings, and speak most fluently when the listener is out of sight. Several parrots kept together will learn to talk by imitating one another, and one of the drollest things I have heard is a pair of African Greys carrying on a conversation composed of various phrases they have learned, interspersed with bursts of very human laughter.

Rivalling the Grey Parrot in talking ability are the Amazons from tropical South America. Whereas the Grey has only one other close relative, the Amazons are a group comprising a number of species all mainly green in colour, with touches of red, yellow or blue in their plumage. The Blue-fronted Amazon is as well known as any. Not only a good talker but a very handsome bird, it is bright green with a blue and yellow forehead, and has splashes of red and blue in the wings. It makes a tame and affectionate pet.

The Indian Ring-necked parakeet is another favourite. Very common in India, it has been tamed since Roman times, and incidentally breeds freely in captivity both in Europe and America. Not a very good talker, it can however be taught many amusing tricks. The common form is apple green with a red beak and a pink and black ring round its neck. Aviculturists have now succeeded in breeding two beautiful colour varieties — one yellow and the other powder blue. Unlike Greys and Amazonas which have short tails the Ring-neck, being a parakeet, has a long tapering tail.

Many other kinds of parrots are kept as pets. If tame they make good companions and most learn to say a few words. The well known cockatoos — white with yellow or orange crests — and macaws — the largest of all parrots and also the most gaudily coloured in scarlet, yellow, green and blue — are sometimes kept in private homes, but their loud voices and destructive beaks make them unsuitable inmates of the average household.

A talking bird which has gained great popularity in recent years is the Hill Mynah, hand-reared specimens of which surpass most parrots in powers of mimicry. They have one advantage in that they are not shy of talking in front of people — a thing which most parrots are loath to do. Hill Mynahs or Grackles are insectivorous and fruit eating birds which come from India and Malaya. They are distant relatives of starlings and crows — in fact they somewhat resemble a small crow in appearance, being glossy black in plumage with yellow legs, orange beak and yellow flaps of skin on either side of the head. Only hand-reared birds are any good as talkers and pets. Young birds are taken from the nests by the Asians and hand-reared for export to Europe and America.

The cage of the pet house bird should be in a position where it gets plenty of light but is out of draughts. Places to be avoided are in front of a window or between a door and a window. The temperature of the average living room is quite adequate but if it gets very cold at night it is advisable to cover the cage with a piece of cloth.

Make sure that the right kind of food, if the bird is an insectivorous one, is given. This sounds elementary but whereas most pet shops will give the right advice a few may not know as much as they should. A bird can die of starvation in the midst of apparent plenty if it is not given the right food. There are several booklets on this subject on the market, or *Cage & Aviary Birds*, the weekly journal devoted to the bird fancy, runs an advice column which will answer almost any query.

Small birds eat spasmodically all day so their food and water pots should never be allowed to run empty, especially in the evening when they like to fill their crops to last them through the night. A hungry bird will quickly get a chill and die. Canaries, finches, Budgerigars and parrots shell their seed before eating it, swallowing only the kernel and

Parrots are expensive but popular and long-lived pets. Many become very good 'talkers', simply because they are good mimics and not because they have the faintest idea of the real meaning of the words they pick up. This African Grey Parrot is a most beautiful bird, with a grey-blue back and red tail.

Mynahs are found mainly in southern Asia. They are not related at all to parrots but are large members of the great family of starlings. Like many of their tribe, they have remarkable powers of mimicry and the best birds, which make better 'talkers' than most parrots, are very valuable.

leaving the husk. To the uninitiated what appears to be a pot full of seed may in fact only contain empty husks.

Besides their seed and water these birds require fresh greenfood such as lettuce, chickweed or dandelion two or three times a week, coarse sand on the cage floor to facilitate cleaning and to provide them with grit, and a piece of cuttlefish bone stuck between the wires of the cage for them to nibble.

Cages should be cleaned out about twice a week and perches should be so arranged that the birds do not catch their tails when they turn round. Bathing is important and should be allowed two or three times a week. Canaries and finches will bathe themselves in a saucer of water or one of the specially made bird baths that hang on the open door of the cage. Budgerigars and parrots should be sprayed with clean water. Special bird sprayers can be purchased quite cheaply or an old scent spray with the hole in the nozzle slightly enlarged will serve the purpose.

Provided the bird is tame enough it should be allowed out of its cage whenever its owner is on hand to keep an eye on it. A bird which is not tame enough to return to its cage of its own free will should not be kept in a cage at all; its proper place is in an aviary with others of its own kind. Close the windows and guard the fires when your pet is loose in the room.

The average life span of a Canary or Budgerigar is about ten years and that of a parrot about twenty-five years. Many exceed these figures but, like ourselves, birds do not all reach their allotted span.